- A NOVEL INSPIRED BY ACTUAL EVENTS -

Men in My Town

KEITH SMITH

ISBN: 1-4392-2625-3
ISBN-13: 9781439226254
LCCN: 2009900598

Visit www.booksurge.com to order additional copies.

Dedicated to masked men and superheroes,
real and imagined.

Chapter 1

We pulled into the empty parking lot behind the Mobil gas station next to Cote's Meat Market on Higginson Avenue. He took the keys from the ignition and got out. I sat motionless as he walked behind the car, came around to the passenger side, unlocked the door and slowly walked away. He walked in front of the car, turned left and was near the driver's front fender when I pulled open my door and jumped out. I stood in the parking lot looking straight at him, fearing what might happen if I let him out of my sight. Time stood still. I was standing on the passenger side of the car; he was standing on the driver's side, the car between us offering me five feet of safety. With his head down, never looking in my direction, he just opened the driver's door to his shitty little car and got in.

I was terrified and furious at the same time. I bent down, picked up a piece of broken cement from one of those blocks you pull up to at the front of a parking spot, and threw it against the hatchback window of the purple AMC Gremlin. I had to leave a mark. I had to be able to prove to the cops that it was this guy, in this car. The sound of shattering glass reassured me and no doubt angered him beyond rage.

All I had to do was cross Higginson Avenue, get through the bowling alley parking lot, up the hill behind the back of the building and down Middle Street, three blocks to home. I ran into traffic and kept running, never looking back, running to get away, running to get home, running away to stay alive.

Every breath was a deep breath, filling my lungs with rapid bursts of cold March air. My heart was pounding; my pulse was racing. I was scared, terrified, hysterical, crying, trembling and in pain. Every sense was heightened. Sounds were magnified. Lights were brighter. I could hear the motor on the giant rotating bowling pin as the glowing neon *Lincoln Lanes* sign lit up the corner of Higginson Avenue.

I ran down the sloping driveway of the bowling alley, across the parking lot and to the back of the building. This part of town was familiar and safe territory for me. My friends and I played back here. We rode our bikes up and down the hill that rose up to the dead end of Middle Street. We played one-man tennis here, hitting balls against the back of the bowling alley. We hit golf balls in the sand, the younger boys making believe we were in the world's largest sand trap, while the older guys hung out in their cars, drinking beer and rolling dice. But making it up the hill this night seemed impossible. I ran, lost my balance, tripping over my own feet, falling face first to the ground. I got up, stumbled and fell again and began crawling on my hands and knees. I had to keep moving. Moving toward home. I was losing time and distance. Had he come after me? Was he chasing me through the parking lot? Was he coming up the hill? Where was he? Who was he?

My hands were bleeding from crawling on the hard, frozen sand. I made it to the top of the hill and into Greg's back yard, but I was too ashamed and embarrassed to go to his house for help. I had to get home. I just needed to get home. I was exhausted. I ran up the street past Ricky's house and started hiding behind trees, crouching behind parked cars to rest and catch my breath. Why was it so hard to get away? Why was it taking so long to go such a short distance? Where was everybody? Why wasn't anyone who could help me on the street?

Then I heard a car. I was sure that it was him. I was sure he was looking for me, tracking me down. He must have thought he'd gotten away with what he'd done, until I broke the rear window. How was he going to explain that? It had to be him coming back to find me, to beat me, to kill me. I was being hunted in a very real game of deadly hide-and-go-seek. I had stayed alive tonight but now I was about to die on the street six houses from home. His car was coming. *Use your head,* I thought.

I lay on my belly and crawled under the rear bumper of a Ford Galaxie parked on Middle Street. A few more feet, and I was wedged between the rear tires. He wouldn't find me there. In a fetal position with my head resting on my right arm, I lay under the Ford, praying for the car to pass.

All I could see were the tires of the approaching car. What a mistake. How was I to know if it really was the guy in the purple Gremlin or not? As the car rolled through the intersection of Meader and Middle Street, my hiding spot suddenly became suffocating. I realized I'd made a mistake crawling under this car. I wasn't safe at all. If he found me here, I'd be trapped. It was impossible to move. I could hear and feel my pulse beating in my head. The headlights were blinding: I couldn't see the car, couldn't make out whether it was the Gremlin, couldn't know for sure whether it was him or not. Did the headlights coming toward me light up the Galaxie parked on the side of the road? Could the driver see me under this car? Was it him? *Does the son-of-a-bitch know I'm here? If he stops, I'm screwed.*

I watched the front tires and then the back tires roll by, as the car continued north up Middle Street. Paralyzed with fear, I lay motionless under the car in the dark of the night, on the cold, frozen street.

I had to get home. A few moments after the car passed, I shimmied my body to get out from under the Galaxie. It was much more difficult getting out than it had been crawling under. Maybe the need to hide had blinded me to the reality of how difficult it was to crawl under the car just a few minutes ago. As I brushed up against the undercarriage of the Galaxie, my jacket got caught and I bumped my head hard. All I could see was the dark street underneath me. My hands hurt. It took forever, arms and legs scraping against the cold road, my head banging against the bottom of the car. I finally struggled out onto the street. I stood up and started running.

I made it one block. Then it happened again. This time at the corner of South Street and Middle Street. A different car or the same car? Had the first car doubled back? Was it a neighbor coming home or the asshole in the Gremlin looking to find me, to silence me, to kill me? Hiding under the Galaxie, I'd learned that I needed to see what was going on, to move, to run, to fight. I wasn't going to make the same mistake again.

The large old house on the corner of Middle and South Street had a big back yard and beautiful hedges lining the property. I crawled under the hedge to hide while the car came toward me. I was one house away from home, burrowing deep into the base of the hedge like an animal, eyes wide open, pulse racing, heart pounding, trying to blend in with the bushes and the darkness of the night. It was cold, the ground was frozen, and sticks from the hedge were scratching and cutting my face. Pressing my body to the ground, and deep into the hedge, I had good cover. I was out of sight, but I could see. I was stationary but could get up and move, run, fight if I needed to. Again, I heard a silent scream in my head. *Where is everybody? Why isn't there anyone on the street who can help me?*

I was terrified. All alone. Filled with fear. Sweating in the winter cold. The car stopped at the intersection, just out of view to my right. "Jesus Christ, when will this end?" I whispered. I wasn't swearing. I was a Catholic boy praying. Heart pounding, I watched the wood-paneled Ford LTD station wagon roll through the intersection heading east on South Street. Thank God.

It was March 1, 1974, around 8:00 in the evening. I was fourteen years old and weighed 110 pounds. Over the past hour and a half, I had been abducted, beaten and raped by a total stranger. But I was home now and I was alive.

He went home to the rented first floor apartment he shared with his wife in the two-story tenement. As he walked up the porch steps, the twin eight year old boys who lived on the second floor, innocent and unaware of his obsession, playfully ran past him, up the stairs and into their apartment. He was filled with anger, anxiety, worry, concern, apprehension, angst and fear. *The son-of-a-bitch broke my rear window*, he thought to himself. How would he explain being late and the broken hatchback window to his wife? *Fuck her, I don't owe her an explanation.*

He came in the house, mumbled something about working late and that someone broke the hatchback window of his car. He moped around the apartment for a few minutes, then locked himself in a bedroom.

Why did I do it again, he asked himself as he sat on their bed. *Why can't I stop?* He was aware of the risk, the danger, the inevitable knock on the door by the police, the embarrassing flashing red lights in front of his house, the condescending interrogation by the detectives, followed by jail, bail, court and the threat of prison. It was only a matter of time.

His wife sensed something was terribly wrong, and she had a strong suspicion that he had hurt another boy. His behavior was the same each time. He was brooding again, visibly agitated and angry. He came home, said nothing, took a shower and washed his clothes. It was the only time he did his own laundry.

The first time it happened, he didn't bother her. The cops came and he simply walked out the front door of their modest apartment with his hands cuffed behind his back. When she suspected he had done it again, the second time, she questioned him. He answered her questions by punching her in the face, a closed left fist leaving her with a black eye and a cut on her right cheek.

The third time, he didn't wait for her questions. When the cops pulled up and knocked on their door, he began beating her as if she was responsible for what he had done. The cops broke through the door and pulled him off, throwing him a beating as they cuffed him and dragged him out onto the porch and into the cruiser.

She didn't want to be home when the cops came this time; it was the only way she'd be safe. She had to leave before he became violent toward her again. She left the apartment silently, without saying anything to her boy-raping husband and walked down Washington Street to a friend's apartment.

When he was last released from prison he swore to himself, his wife and his attorney that he'd change. Yet in less than four months, he did it again. He didn't change, he wouldn't change, he couldn't change. He was compelled to repeat his despicable, criminal sexual behavior. There was no stopping the overwhelming, uncontrollable compulsion that drove him to hunt, beat and sexually assault young boys, not even the threat of prison.

The thought of prison was all encompassing and oppressive. He began breathing deeply as the initial stages of a panic attack came over him. He couldn't go back to prison. If the kid went to the cops and they came for him, it would be inevitable, only a matter of time, perhaps a few months at most, before he was back doing time. The overcrowded cells, the smell of urine, the lack of privacy, the beatings, the sex, the screams, the sleeplessness, the sense of powerlessness, forced obedience to others, being dominated by older, stronger prisoners and prison guards, the dreadful food—it was too much. Prison was unbearable. Going back was unthinkable. His breathing became increasingly labored as thoughts of prison raced through his head. *I can't go back to the ACI. I should have killed the kid.*

Chapter 2

I was a right defenseman on the Lincoln Red Wings, a hockey team in the town's recreational league for boys between 14 and 18 years old. In a year, Lincoln High School would have its first hockey team and many of the players in the rec league would find themselves representing Lincoln on the ice. I didn't get to play defense because I was big–just the opposite. I was young and small for my age but could skate backward better than most, and that was a valuable skill when the other team had the puck and was skating toward your goalie.

Our coach held team meetings at the barbershop he owned on Front Street. We reviewed the past few games, going over what we did right, what we did wrong, what the other team did that we could learn from. We reviewed our plays, discussed strategy for the next game and congratulated each player for a goal scored or assist made in the past

game. It was a good group of kids led by two dear men who
put a great deal of time and energy into helping kids have
fun, develop as young athletes and enjoy life.

There was a team meeting this night and I was walking home after the meeting. I wasn't just walking home; I
was hitchhiking. A purple AMC Gremlin pulled over, the
passenger door opened and I got in. I told the guy I was
looking to go up Smithfield Avenue to Hartley's Pork Pies.
I know what you're thinking: The kid never should have
been hitchhiking, and what's Hartley's Pork Pies?

Hartley's is a family-owned business, selling pork pies
in the Fairlawn section in the south end of Lincoln. It's
been operating out of a small red brick building on the
corner of Smithfield Avenue and Meader Street for over
70 years. There's always a sign in the window, with either
the *"Yes We Have Pies"* side showing or the other side, a
major disappointment to people who drove a long distance for the chance to buy a pork pie, *"Closed."* You see,
Hartley's isn't open till 5 p.m. every day. When I was a
kid, Mr. Hartley baked a certain number of pork pies in
the morning and when they were gone, he'd close. If he
sold out by 11 a.m., the front door got locked at 11 and
he'd flip the *"Yes We Have Pies"* sign. If he sold out by 2
p.m., you might have been lucky enough to have a pork
pie for lunch.

When you open the front door of Hartley's, you walk
into to a scene right out of the back streets of London. Pictures of Queen Elizabeth II and Winston Churchill are on
the wall alongside aging, faded maps of Britain. There are
no tables or chairs and every order is "to go." You stand

at the counter, place your order, collect your pies in their signature brown box, pay and leave.

Hartley's makes a handmade pie of ground pork mixed with spices and a raised letter "H" baked into the top crust. The pies are small enough to hold in one hand. It's a local culinary treat with fans throughout New England, and it's not uncommon to see cars and trucks parked in front of Hartley's with license plates from as far away as New York and New Jersey. When I wasn't there to buy pies for lunch or dinner, which we did at least once a week, I hung out on Hartley's steps to catch the morning school bus.

As he drove past Hartley's, I told him I'd get out at the Fairlawn Fire Station, a couple hundred feet past Hartley's. He said nothing and drove past the fire station. I told him to pull over and he remained silent. I realized I was in trouble but had no idea what he had planned, no idea what I was in for. I remember telling him if I didn't get home, people would be looking for me. He remained silent and continued to drive south on Smithfield Avenue toward Pawtucket.

Now I was scared. What was going on? Who was this asshole? Why didn't he stop at Hartley's or the fire station? Why was he not letting me out of his shitty little car? Where was he going? Where was he taking me and why?

He was slowing down to take a right onto Grafton Street, and I realized this was my chance to get away. As he turned the corner, I pulled the door handle and leaned hard against the door, hoping to fall out of the car and roll into the street in front of the parking lot of Kiernan's bar. The door didn't open. The knobs on the door locks had been removed and the door couldn't be opened from the inside with the locks down, hidden out of sight, just below the top of the passenger side door panel. I rolled the window down and began to yell, hoping the kids sitting on the wall at the Lindsey Tavern would hear me scream for help.

That's when I felt my face explode. I had been punched hard in the face. This wasn't a hockey-gloved punch to my helmeted head delivered by a teenage hockey player. This was an adult male, turning to the right, squaring his shoulders, and throwing a clenched left fist into the left side of my face, knocking my head against the passenger door and blurring my vision. He told me if I did anything like that again, he'd kill me. I believed him, so I began noticing little things, things I'd need to tell the police, because I knew if I could stay alive tonight, there would be no way this asshole was going to get away with hurting me. The first thing I noticed was that he was left-handed.

He continued to drive in silence. As long as he was driving, I was safe. If and when he stopped, I'd be at risk. I still had no idea what he intended to do or why I was being abducted; I just needed to keep my wits about me, keep him from punching me in the face again and stay alive. He drove up Cobble Hill Road and took a right onto Louisquisset Pike. As we drove past the State Police barracks, I remember praying for a Trooper to pull out from the station as he began his tour or to have a Trooper come up behind us, returning to the barracks. If I could get a Trooper behind us, I'd create a commotion in the car that would get his attention and this would be over. It didn't happen.

We continued up Louisquisset Pike toward the entrance to Lincoln Woods State Park. It was nighttime and I remember thinking, *If he takes me into Lincoln Woods, he's going to kill me.* My heart's racing as we continue toward the entrance. Horrible thoughts about how I'm going to die fill my head. He drives past the entrance to Lincoln Woods and continues up Louisquisset Pike. Thank God.

He takes a right onto Breakneck Hill Road, a left onto Great Road, a left onto Sherman Avenue and another left, about 100 feet down a dirt road. He shuts off the car and gets out. I have no idea what's coming next. I'm in way over my head. I'm scared, I'm alone, and I'm terrified as he walks around the car. There's no one around. No one to help. What does this guy want with me? He looked harmless when I got into the car. He's wearing a maroon blazer, for Christ's sake. He unlocks the passenger door from the outside and tells me to get out. I panic and try to crawl over the driver's seat to get away. He reaches in and grabs me by the foot and begins dragging me across the seats, trying to get me out of the car. I'm kicking at his arms and hands, trying to break away. He reaches into the car, grabs me by the collar of my jacket and pulls me upright in the passenger seat. In an instant he slips a belt over my head, around my neck and drags me from the car, like a disobedient dog on a choke collar. With the belt tightening around my neck, I'm choking, losing consciousness as I'm being dragged out of the car. Gasping for air as the belt tightens around my neck, I'm 14 years old, alone and helpless, unable to fight back, 100 feet deep in the cold, dark woods off of Sherman Avenue being beaten and raped by a serial pedophile. *Stay alive,* I thought. *Stay alive, and he won't get away with doing this to you.*

I went to the Lincoln Police station with my father and my brother. It was around 8:15 p.m. There was a genuine look of empathy on the face of the desk cop as I tried to explain what had happened to me in the past few hours. A detective came out front and took us to a tiny, windowless, nondescript office in the basement of the police station. I told the detective my story. I was a 14-year-old kid who only minutes ago thought he was being hunted down and would be killed in the streets around his home by the man that had beaten and raped me on the other side of town. My father and brother were visibly filled with anger and contempt. The detective was a seasoned cop, all business, no emotion and his questions were direct.

"No, I don't know who he is."

"No, I've never seen him before."

"Yes, I can give you a description."

I had a good physical description of the guy and his car. Thirtyish, shoulder-length reddish-brown hair, side-burns, tan pants, maroon blazer, white shirt. Purple AMC Gremlin with a white stripe, white interior. There should be scratches on the right side of the passenger seat, scratches I put there to leave my mark. There was no knob on the passenger door lock. I knew his license plate number. When I was in the car, I read it on the back of the inspection sticker located in the lower right hand corner of his windshield. From the moment he threw his first punch into my face, I knew he was left-handed. I had his fingerprints on the $10 bill he gave me, and oh, by the way, I shattered his hatchback window with a chunk of cement. It should be easy to find his car. And it was. Within an hour, the detective told us they were bringing a guy in for questioning. They had him. I was alive, and he wasn't going to get away with what he had done to me.

The detective started the recorder on the other side of the two-way mirror, then walked into the interview room. From the very beginning, the suspect denied everything. He offered a bullshit explanation for the shattered hatch-back window on his car, which at that very moment was being hooked up to a tow truck and impounded as evidence. The police caught him in one lie after another and in less than twenty minutes, they had enough to arrest Ronald Thomas Kohl, age 29, a serial pedophile with a previous record of sex offenses and prison time.

Chapter 3

In 1974, Mayor Joe Doorley, Jr. was losing control of City
Hall. In November, Vincent "Buddy" Cianci, prosecutor
of the Rhode Island Attorney General's Anti-Corruption
Strike Force, would be elected Mayor by a margin of only
709 votes, receiving 26,832 votes to Doorley's 26,123.
Cianci, the first Italian-American Mayor, effectively put an
end to more than a century of Irish Democrat rule over the
City of Providence.

Cianci served as Mayor of Providence twice, from 1975
to 1984 and again from 1991 to 2002. His 21-year reign
came to an end when he was convicted on a single charge
of conspiracy after being acquitted on 42 of 43 charges,
including bribery, extortion and mail fraud. During Cianci's early years in office, Providence benefited from over
$600 million of Community Development money used to
finance a grand plan to revitalize downtown. The Amtrak

and Conrail train tracks were rerouted 700 feet to the north, just south of the State House, and the three rivers running through the heart of the city were redirected, opening over 70 acres of prime, developable land in downtown Providence. Hotels, apartments, condominiums, restaurants, office space, clubs, cafes, galleries and retail stores filled the newly reclaimed land, creating jobs and giving people a reason to go downtown. The revitalization of downtown Providence during Cianci's administration led to an economic renaissance, reversing decades of urban decay, and put Providence on the map as a destination city for Rhode Islanders, visitors, vacationers and conventioneers.

Providence is rich in history, academia and the arts. It's home of the Ivy League's Brown University, Rhode Island School of Design, Providence College and Johnson & Wales. It has a booming Arts & Entertainment district, with studios and production facilities for artists, writers, directors and sculptors. There's the Providence Performing Arts Center, Trinity Repertory Company and WaterFire, the award-winning performance art installation by Barnaby Evens, with 100 bonfires on the city's three rivers, responsible for drawing over 10 million visitors to Providence's Waterplace Park and the streets of Downcity Providence.

Today's Renaissance City is not the Providence of old. In the mid-'70s the streets around Kennedy Plaza, located between City Hall and the John O. Pastore Federal Building, bustling during the day with bankers from Industrial National Bank, executives from Textron and insurance brokers with offices in the Turks Head Building, were taken over after sunset by low-life street criminals, common thugs of the mugger variety, male, female and transvestite prostitutes and drug dealers selling pot, hash, Quaaludes, mescaline and heroin. There was a booming sex trade, with movie houses, bookstores, peepshows, prostitutes, sex clubs and dingy topless bars operating in the few blocks between City Hall and Saint Peter & Paul Cathedral, the home of the Diocese of Providence.

Providence after dark wasn't a place for the innocent or virtuous. Those who left the city when they got off work for the vanilla suburbs of Cumberland, Lincoln, Cranston, Warwick, East Greenwich, Barrington and Newport knew it and so did the people who drove into Providence after dark.

When Ronald Thomas Kohl visited Providence after dark, he went straight for the sex clubs, bars and bookstores off Westminster Street, a couple of blocks behind City Hall. He was a regular, cruising the adult bookstores on Saturday nights. Tonight was no different, but this night, as Kohl drove into Providence, he was being followed. As he took the Atwells Avenue exit, he was being followed. As he drove past the Holiday Inn and the Providence Police Station, he was being followed. As he went up Fountain Street and took a right onto Beverly, he was being followed. As he parked his shitty little AMC Gremlin on Washington Street, he was being followed. As he entered the adult bookstore on Snow Street, he was being followed. As he left and cruised the streets and alleys looking for sex, he was being followed, and all the while, he was unaware that a bookie in Lincoln had put the word out that he wanted to know everything there was to know about Ronald Thomas Kohl.

Chapter 4

Mike was a first generation American, the son of a dockworker from the seaside town of Latakia on the Mediterranean coast of Syria. On the street he was known as The Syrian. He lived in Lincoln and ran his bookmaking business out of a second floor apartment above a hamburger joint on Dexter Street in Central Falls. He made a good living collecting $10 and $20 bets from guys in the neighborhood who couldn't get to the track or who wanted to bet their favorite sports team or play the daily number.

No one knows the daily number anymore. Before state-sponsored lotteries, you could place a bet with a bookie on the daily number. Unlike the ping-pong balls you see being pulled out of a machine on the evening news, the daily number was the last three dollar amounts, in reverse order, of the total amount wagered at Lincoln Downs. If the gamblers who left their rent money and social security checks at the track bet a total of $45,087 for the day, the daily number would be 780: the last three numbers of the daily take, in reverse order. So on any given day, before the track closed, you could visit or call your bookie and pick any three-digit number and pray for good luck. If you bet the number 780 yesterday and this morning's sports page showed the total amount bet at Lincoln Downs was any amount with the last three whole dollars being 087, you won. Yes, the editors of the local paper were complicit and cooperated with bookies and bettors by printing the daily take at local tracks. This information in the sports page sold more newspapers in the towns around Lincoln Downs than the front-page headlines.

The Syrian's second floor office offered a little bit of protection from the police—not the Central Falls police, but the State Police who would periodically raid his operation. It took time for the State Troopers to get up the stairs to the second floor, and in the bookmaking business, a few seconds could mean the difference between going to jail and just having to replace the front door, which the cops always knocked off the hinges, even when the door was unlocked.

In the '60s and '70s Mike actually used rice paper to record bets. On a few occasions, he was able to use the time it took the police to run up the stairs to dissolve his rice paper betting slips in the 20-gallon fish tank he kept on a table at the side of his desk. Bookmaking was hard to prove without evidence, and when the police busted down the door and did arrest him, Mike usually spent one night in jail, pled guilty to the misdemeanor charge and paid a fine. He viewed the broken doors, the days out of work, the nights in jail, the arrests and fines as the cost of doing business. Retailers have to finance inventory. Bookies in Central Falls have to pay bribes or fines and buy new doors.

Mike and my Dad grew up on Hunt Street in Central Falls. As young boys they hung out together almost every day, playing in Jenks Park and fishing in Valley Falls Pond. In their teens they did their fair share of hanging out on Hunt Street, Dexter Street and Broad Street and occasionally would get in street fights with kids from Pawtucket who came into Central Falls to raise hell, cause trouble and date the girls. They were good kids, never looking for a fight but never walking away from an opportunity to tussle. When they were a little bit older, both men found themselves fighting North Korean Communists, my father aboard the USS Oglethorpe and Mike on the ground as a Private First Class, USMC, 1st Marine Division.

Both men sailed into Korea on September 15, 1950, when Joint Task Force Seven, with 320 warships and 70,000 men, landed behind enemy lines at Inchon Harbor, one of the most dangerous places on earth to attack from sea. The first troops came ashore at Wolmi-do, led by the 3rd Battalion, 5th Marines. Moving their attack inland, the 5th was joined by their brothers in the 1st Marine Division and the U. S. Army's 32nd Infantry. Over the next week, they advanced towards Seoul, one day at a time in brutal hand-to-hand, house-to-house street combat, finally taking control of Seoul on September 25. With North Korean command of the Pusan region broken, the Communists retreated. 566 UN troops were killed and over 2,700 wounded. The

North Korean People's Army lost more than 35,000 men. The Battle of Inchon, referred to as MacArthur's "Master- stroke," remains one of the most daring feats in military history. Semper Fi, Uncle Mike.

Their fathers were close friends and worked together making light bulbs at Corning Glass Works. Back then, everybody's father, uncle, grandfather or brother made light bulbs at Corning. Operating three shifts and making tens of millions of light bulbs a year, Corning was a major employer in this little city of only one-and-a-half square miles. In Central Falls, where everyone really did know each other, you either worked at Corning Glass or lived next door to someone who did.

Central Falls was always a city populated by the latest wave of immigrants. Back then it was the Irish, the English and the Syrians. Over time it would be Southeast Asians from Viet Nam, Laos and Cambodia, then Central Ameri- cans from Mexico, Columbia and Guatemala. Immigrants and their first generation American kids stayed very close to family and friends and built strong, lifelong relation- ships based on their common struggle for a good life in the United States.

The friendship and bond between my family and Mike's runs three generations deep, and when I saw him in public, people wondered how the Smith kid from Lincoln got away with calling the man everyone knew as The Syrian, "Uncle Mike."

Chapter 5

Unlike what's shown in the movies, violence is very rare in the bookmaking business. Busting someone up over a few hundred dollars is unnecessary and bad for business. Bookies in and around my town knew their bettors personally. They drank in the same bars, went to the same church and spent time together in the bleachers at their kid's little league games. The bettors lived in the same neighborhood for years, many of them still living within a few blocks of where they grew up. Skipping town was out of the question, and the chance of bumping into your bookie while you were running errands, at the car wash or buying groceries was high.

So while you wouldn't wake up with your jaw wired shut or have your kneecaps whacked with a baseball bat, if you came up too short for too long, you'd have a conversation with one of the guys that worked special situations for The Syrian. Kevin was one of those guys. If you were in too deep and couldn't pay The Syrian, you might find yourself listening to Kevin as he suggested you steal a car, break into a tractor trailer at the loading docks or give a beating to someone who deserved one for something more serious than owing a bookie a few hundred dollars.

Kevin's day job was in an auto body shop owned by his older brother. He drove a tow truck and was pretty good at disassembling cars. The tow truck allowed Kevin to bid on municipal towing contracts. Not that you've given it much thought, but when a town cop puts you in the back seat of his Crown Vic and has your car towed, or when there's an accident and a few cars need to be hauled away after the glass is swept up, the police dispatcher calls a tow truck from a list of authorized towing companies. Tow truck owners like the work because they get to earn a few extra bucks by charging towing and storage fees. In 1974, long before Sunshine Laws forced municipalities to seek competitive bids, Kevin figured out that for $100 cash and 15 minutes with the Director of Public Works, you could get on the list.

Kevin didn't just tow cars when the police dispatcher called him out to tow away a wreck. His Hook and Chain tow truck was the perfect cover for a car thief. When he needed money, Kevin would drive through Pawtucket and when he found what he was looking for, pull up in front of the car, turn on the flashing roof lights and with unbridled bravado, hook it up, tow it away, take it to the auto body and strip it for parts. His favorite spots to 'jack cars were supermarkets, restaurants and hospital parking lots. You'd walk into the A&P to buy groceries and when you came out 30 minutes later, your car was gone. Towed away. No one asked any questions. No one noticed anything unusual. Nothing out of the ordinary about a tow truck towing a car from a parking lot, now is there?

Back in the shop, his skill at disassembling automobiles came in handy. The sum of the parts of a Cadillac–the bumpers, rims, tires, doors, fenders, windshield, rear window, leather seats, radio with 8-track, axles, transmission, head lights, brake lights, front grille and engine parts–were always worth more than the whole. Selling the parts was easy. Some he kept for the auto body, others were sold to used car dealers, repair shops, junkyards and scrap metal yards in Pawtucket, Providence and Cranston. Bribing municipal officials for towing contracts, legitimately towing cars for the cops, stealing cars with a tow truck, stripping cars for parts–all in a day's work.

Kevin was a good kid–or a bad kid, depending on your relationship with him. If you were his victim, he was a bad kid. If he was your friend, it couldn't be better. He was smart, loyal, a trained boxer, a tough street fighter, loved his mother and kept his mouth shut. His escapades were his to keep quiet, not something to boast or brag about. Many knuckleheads had been picked up for questioning because they couldn't keep quiet after two too many beers. Eventually someone who overheard them boast about a job they'd done would give up Knucklehead's name as barter to walk away from a simple misdemeanor drug charge. Not Kevin.

Kevin bet with the Syrian and over the years, they got to know each other well. The Syrian loved boxing and he and Kevin would talk for hours about Muhammad Ali,

George Foreman, Joe Frazier and Ken Norton. One day Kevin dropped in unexpectedly and found two guys arguing loudly with the Syrian. He walked in hearing a lot of "fuck you's" being thrown around, and without a word, Kevin walked up to the bigger of the two and cold-cocked him in the head. The guy dropped to the floor without a sound as Kevin's clenched right fist crashed into the chump's head just below the temple. The smaller of the two, standing silently, didn't dare speak and began dragging the unconscious big guy down two flights of stairs to Dexter Street. It's moments like this that made the relationship between Kevin and The Syrian special.

Today was like any other day. Kevin stopped by to pay off what he lost last week, fed the fish in the Syrian's 20-gallon fish tank and pulled up the second of only two chairs in the office. The Syrian asked Kevin if he had some time to do him a favor and if he wanted to make $20 bucks. The Syrian explained that he wanted Kevin to sit in front of an adult bookstore and discourage people from going in. The Syrian wrote the address on a rice paper betting slip and handed it to Kevin, along with four five dollar bills.

Kevin walked over to Ronald Kohl's bookstore in Central Falls carrying a Kodak 110 Instamatic camera and a baseball bat he got from the Syrian. It didn't take long before a middle-aged guy began making his way down the sidewalk, heading toward Kohl's front door. Kevin took out the camera and snapped a picture of the guy. A stocky,

6-foot plus Irish kid with a camera and a baseball bat was enough to make the guy turn around and walk away from a place where he shouldn't have been in the first place. The same scene repeated itself for the next three hours as middle-aged men, old men and older men had their pictures taken as soon as Kevin was sure they were heading for the front door of Kohl's bookstore. Every one of them retreated without a word. Kevin thought it was hilarious. Business was at a standstill, literally. Kevin was having fun, the work was easy, and $20 bucks was $20 bucks. He stayed until the film ran out, photographing and turning back 24 customers before bringing a six-pack of Narragansett cans back to The Syrian's office. Kevin looked forward to telling him about the last few hours and about the undercover cop who was watching the adult bookstore from the front seat of his parked, unmarked Plymouth Fury.

Kevin never asked The Syrian why he wanted him to do what he did or who owned the bookstore. He was smart enough to know when to not ask questions. Kevin finished a beer, placed a $2 bet on 347, and left the Kodak 110 Instamatic camera with The Syrian.

In four days The Syrian knew the names, addresses, phone numbers, marital status, license plate numbers, car descriptions, and occupations of 15 of the 24 men photographed on their way into Ronald Kohl's adult bookstore. The Syrian was confident he'd have information on the other nine within a few days, and six of the current 15 held real promise. You never know when you might be able to use an insurance adjuster, an IRS examiner, a loan officer at Dexter Credit Union, a doctor, a supervisor at the Department of Motor Vehicles or the owner of a funeral home in Pawtucket.

Chapter 6

Kohl's business was really just a large indoor magazine stand catering openly to heterosexuals and discreetly to homosexuals, S & M aficionados and pedophiles. His shelves were lined with recent copies of *Playboy, Penthouse, Oui, Gallery, Screw, Genesis* and *Club International*. In 1974 he was proud to be one of the first stores in Rhode Island to offer Larry Flynt's hardcore magazines, *Hustler* and *Beaver Hunt*. For the guys that liked guys, *Playgirl* was offered alongside *Bronc, Chicken Delight, Rugged, Nude Reflections* and *The Boy Friends*. The *Cosmo* centerfold of a nude Burt Reynolds was framed and nailed to the wall behind the cash register. Fetish magazines catering to the S & M crowd were available under the counter and child pornography was locked away, along with several 8mm films he held in storage.

Kohl had three peep show booths at the back of his store, really just plywood-covered sheetrock partitions where customers would watch loops of eight millimeter porn films. At 25 cents for two minutes on a movie that ran 10 to 20 minutes, there were a lot of quarters to bag at the end of a day. The porn business in general, and the peep show booths in particular, were lucrative and the coin income was almost impossible for the IRS to know about. The $20 to $30 a day, which was easy to avoid paying income tax on, was a tempting horde of cash for income tax evasion and skimming.

When Kohl was released from prison in 1973 he needed a new, safe angle on the sex business. He did time on federal charges of using the mail for the interstate sale of obscene material, related to a mail order business he ran from a house in Central Falls. Kohl was busted by the FBI and the U. S. Postal Police for shipping gay porn magazines, films and pictures of children to buyers in six states. His new peep show booths and 8mm porn films provided Kohl with a business that didn't violate the law, at least not the federal statues related to interstate commerce and the post office. His 8mm film library included copies of *Mona,* a story of a girl who vows to be a virgin until her wedding day, as long as fellatio doesn't count; *School Girl*, a movie involving a three-way sex scene with a married woman who brings home a college girl as a present for her husband; *Behind the Green Door*, with Marilyn Chambers; porn king Gerard Damiano's *Deep Throat* with Linda Lovelace; plus *The Boys in the Sand* and *Bijou*, two films that launched Casey Donovan's gay porn career.

Kohl was a hardcore pervert, a sexual deviant, a pornographer and child molester who was in the sex business for the sex, not just for the money. Before his 28th birthday, he had been arrested for Unnatural Sex Acts, Child Molestation, Promoting Obscenity and Distributing Obscene Material. The federal charges in 1973, for distributing obscene material, put him behind bars and gave the Feds what they needed: a child molester who never wanted to go back to prison and a snitch with valuable connections to the porn production and distribution business in Providence.

In the '70s, the local police had a simple way to deal with most sex crimes that didn't end in murder. They'd bring the perp in for a talk, let him know they would be watching him and on occasion smack the pervert around a little when no one, or everyone, was looking. Local enforcement of obscenity laws was a non-event, left up to the Feds and State Attorney Generals looking to move into the Governor's office during the next election cycle.

On occasion, the Feds would rein in a bad guy with the Capone Strategy. The feds convicted Al Capone on tax evasion because it was easier than proving murder. Convicting pornographers on obscenity charges was difficult, while charging them with income tax evasion, using the mails to distribute obscene material and other federal charges stemming from their involvement in pornography was much easier. The Feds had a vulnerable target in Ronald Kohl, a convict who had done time in prison on obscenity charges, a convict who had been arrested for unnatural sex acts and sex crimes involving children. Kohl didn't want to go back to prison, yet he couldn't help himself. When he was released late in 1973, he went right back to his old ways, running an adult bookstore and stalking young boys.

As the Feds watched Kohl and the men that visited his store, they weren't interested in building another case against Kohl as much as they were in putting pressure on him, pressure that hopefully would lead him to cooperate. They would park directly in front of his store and stand on the sidewalk, drinking coffee in the morning and eating sandwiches for lunch in the afternoon. Their presence and the ever-so-obvious undercover Plymouth Fury cop car with the trunk mounted whip antennas, effectively put an end to customers walking in to spend a few minutes in the store and a few bucks on porn.

The Feds' strategy was to pressure Kohl into giving information on his contacts in the business. Before Kohl's conviction in the early '70s, the recruiting, filming, production, advertising and distribution of pornography throughout the United States was controlled by one guy in Cleveland who got his start distributing comic books and adult magazines. In a few years, the low legal risk and high profits of the porn business captured the attention of organized crime. With the cooperation of the guy from Cleveland, agreements were soon reached to cut the country into three autonomous areas that would control the porn business on a regional basis from Los Angeles, New York and Atlanta.

It wasn't long before people from New York visited the men that ran Providence and started talking about controlling the distribution of pictures, magazines, film and peep show booths throughout Rhode Island and the rest of New England.

In a matter of months, Kohl was no longer an independent bookstore owner. He had new business partners that invited themselves in. He had new suppliers for his magazines and films, a new source of financing that charged more for interest than the local branch of the Dexter Credit Union and a weekly obligation to pay taxes to a guy who didn't work for City Hall or the IRS.

The Feds used simple tactics to fuck with Kohl. Since he did time for sending obscene material through the mail, they followed him to the post office every time he needed a stamp. When he left Central Falls and went to the post office on Front Street in Lincoln, they called Lincoln's detectives for a meet and greet in the post office parking lot.

Their visible presence in front of his store cut down on the number of customers willing to make their presence known to federal agents. With revenue down, surely Kohl's new business partners would think he was skimming. With sales down, his suppliers would think he was getting material from someone else, perhaps even reproducing pictures and films himself. Either way, it would be hard for Kohl to convince the people he was doing business with that their take was down because his revenue in the booming porn business was off. It would only be a matter of time before Kohl was going to feel the squeeze, either from the Feds or his new partners in crime.

Chapter 7

I grew up in the Fairlawn section of the town of Lincoln, 4 miles north of Providence and 4 miles from the Massachusetts border.

My Lincoln was visited by bad luck. I grew up with a blind girl, a deaf boy and a girl and a boy that were both retarded. Kids in my town died from suicide, overdoses, murder and freak accidents. I'm not talking about your typical, run-of-the-mill car accident. No, my friends died horribly, one by falling in the woods and impaling himself through the neck on a small tree stump and another by falling into the prop of an airplane after pulling on the propeller to jumpstart a single engine plane. A dwarf teenage girl was raped and murdered. Steven OD'd, and was found as a floater, tossed into a pond by his junkie asshole buddies. Another kid, a heroin overdose, froze to death in the playground 500 feet from my parents' front door.

There was a great cast of characters in my neighborhood and my life. There was the gas station owner who labeled cheap regular gasoline as expensive premium to steal a few cents a gallon, the owner of the dry cleaner who laundered more than dirty shirts, a supermarket deli worker, retired military, a car mechanic, fuel truck drivers, a tow truck driver, two long-haul truckers, a handful of bartenders, several bar owners, a half-dozen full time drunks, parolees working as roofers, construction workers, a father and son team of prison guards, several factory workers, a factory owner, a state trooper, full-time cops, volunteer firemen, school teachers, a tailor, professional athletes, carpenters, plumbers, a limo driver, garbage men, the insurance broker, an undertaker, the phone company lineman, hustler pool players, drug dealers, elected public officials and a few Catholic priests.

I knew the families that owned big construction companies, trucking companies, and the largest chain of retail liquor stores in Rhode Island. I knew professional wrestlers and racetrack guys, including full time professional gamblers, trainers, grooms and jockeys.

There were young guys and old men that had gone to prison, were in prison, were on parole, would go to prison, would die in prison. Men who carried guns legally and illegally, in their cars, on their hips and men who stuck guns in people's ears. I knew men that had been shot and I'm sure I knew men who'd shot people, although no one talked about that. I knew guys involved in insurance fraud, auto theft, truck hijacking and the guys that broke into tractor-trailers parked at warehouse loading docks. On weekends, I caddied for their lawyers at Kirkbrae Country Club.

While my father knew all the cops and half the cops knew me by name, I knew bookies, bagmen and owners of legitimate businesses that laundered cash. I grew up, hung out, went fishing, played baseball, played hockey and went to school with their kids, their nieces and nephews. The men in my town knew me, liked me, trusted me, watched out for me. They were good men who on occasion did what most people would consider bad things. One thing I know for sure, they did everything they needed to do to keep our neighborhood safe.

It was after nine o'clock on a cold, dark winter night and only a faint light far in the back of Giordano Tailors gave any indication that Dennis was working on a suit. When he heard the glass break, he shut off the lights and slowly pulled back the velvet curtain covering the entrance to his cutting room. From inside his shop he saw the guy reach into the broken driver's side window, open the car door, get in, close the door, bend down and disappear out of sight.

Dennis moved through his darkened front room, out his front door and into the parking lot behind Sportsman's bar. The petty burglar had no idea he had been seen and never heard Dennis approach as he was cutting wires to remove the Craig 8-track cassette player.

Within seconds Dennis was at the driver's side door of the Monte Carlo. He leaned through the broken glass and with both hands grabbed the punk by the collar of his coat. Before he could realize what was happening, he was being pulled headfirst through the broken car window. Halfway through the window, with his head and chest out of the car and his hips and legs still inside, his bowels let loose. This guy literally had the shit scared out of him.

Dennis pinned the guy to the gravel parking lot and held him there with a knee in his back. He lifted the guy's coat and pulled a wallet from the rear pocket of his Levi's. Dennis took the guy's driver's license, yanked him up from the ground, spun him around and pinned him against the car. The license had an address in Pawtucket. Dennis didn't recognize the guy or his last name. Dennis said, "You better know somebody," then asked, "Who do you know?" It was a shame the guy didn't come up with a name.

Dennis dragged him into the bar. Guys were shooting pool, drinking beer and eating fish and chips. Barely two steps into Sportsman's, Dennis asked who owned the yellow Monte Carlo parked out back. The bar went silent and the pool game came to an end. Old men at the bar didn't move, didn't turn around; they stayed put, looking straight ahead into the full wall mirror behind the bar and kept drinking their beer. One guy near the pool table looked up; two other guys, obviously with him, moved toward Dennis. Danny, the owner of Sportsman's, pulled a baseball bat out from under the bar, slammed it against the counter to get everyone's attention and suggested the two guys stay put. Dennis announced this guy had smashed the car's window and tried to steal the radio. Dennis told the thief that he shouldn't even think about going to the cops, rubbed the guy's driver's license in his face and whispered in his ear, "Don't come back. I know where you live." With that, Dennis threw the guy to the floor of the bar and walked back to his shop to finish working on a suit for my Uncle Mike, The Syrian.

Ten minutes went by before Dennis heard the siren. The cops were on scene first, then an ambulance came a minute or two later. No one in the bar had any information for the Lincoln Police about the guy with no identification lying unconscious on the sidewalk in front of Sportsman's.

Chapter 8

Jimmy opened the envelope from Chase Manhattan Bank and carefully unfolded the newly printed stock certificate. The crisp banknote paper with a rose red border, Certificate Number J135-661 for 102 shares of General Motors Corporation felt rich in his hands. He was proud to see his name printed in the middle of the certificate, under the bold print GM banner and the vignette of a GM plant, a train, bus and automobile. Jimmy read, "This is to Certify that MR. JAMES MARONI is the owner of ***ONE HUNDRED TWO*** fully paid and non-assessable shares of the common stock of General Motors Corporation Cusip 370442 10 5. Witness the signatures of the duly authorized officers MARCH 16, 1974." There in the lower right hand corner was the signature of Edward N. Cole, President of General Motors. Jimmy smirked and with no one around to hear him said, "Thank you, Mr. Cole."

With GM bouncing between $50 and $53 3/8 per share, the 102 shares were worth more than $5,000. Jimmy held 4 other GM stock certificates, each one for 102 shares, each one printed on the rich textured banknote paper, each one with a different certificate number, each one with a different date, each one with his name prominently printed in the middle of the certificate with the president of General Motors attesting to Jimmy's ownership. Although he now held 5 certificates, this latest one, the one dated March 16, 1974, was the only certificate that was actually worth anything.

Jimmy originally purchased 102 shares of GM in early 1973 and asked his broker to register and ship the shares so he'd have the physical stock certificate in his possession. Within a week of getting the stock in the mail, Jimmy called his broker at Dean Witter, claiming he never received the certificate. The broker contacted Chase Manhattan Bank, the transfer agent for General Motors, stating the stock certificate never arrived at his client's house. Jimmy filed the necessary paperwork and paid a small fee to have the original certificate cancelled and a replacement certificate issued by Chase.

Transfer Agents are banks hired by corporations to keep detailed records of the names, addresses, social security numbers and number of shares held by a company's investors. GM's Transfer Agent was Chase Manhattan Bank. When Jimmy filed the Lost or Stolen Affidavit and paid a small indemnity fee, Chase cancelled his ownership of the original stock certificate and simply mailed a replacement certificate for 102 shares. Within days of notifying Chase Manhattan, Jimmy had in his possession two stock certificates, the original which he never really lost and the replacement certificate, each for 102 shares. The first one, cancelled on the books of Chase Manhattan, was worthless. The second one, valid on the books of Chase Manhattan, was negotiable, with a market value exceeding $6,000 at the time.

Three months later, Jimmy contacted Chase Manhattan directly and stated that his second certificate had been lost or stolen. They mailed him the papers necessary to file the Lost or Stolen Affidavit and with a small fee paid, Chase went about the process for a second time. They cancelled the second certificate, rendering it worthless, and issued James Maroni a third certificate for 102 shares. Seven days after calling Chase Manhattan bank, Jimmy had his original certificate, the second certificate and now a third stock certificate for 102 shares of General Motors.

Six months later Jimmy did it again. He contacted Chase Manhattan Bank, had the third certificate cancelled and a fourth certificate issued. Four months later, now in March 1974, he did it for the final time, contacting Chase, having the fourth certificate cancelled and having Certificate Number J135-661 for 102 shares of General Motors Corporation registered and shipped to Mr. James Maroni.

With five stock certificates issued by Chase Manhattan Bank over the past year, Jimmy held in his hands what appeared to be 510 shares of General Motors with a market value in excess of $26,000. In reality only the last stock certificate, dated March 16, 1974 was negotiable, each of the previous four certificates having been cancelled on the books of Chase Manhattan Bank. Lucky for Jimmy, only he and Chase Manhattan Bank knew that.

Jimmy walked into the Old Stone Bank on Kennedy Plaza in Providence and filled out a loan application for $20,000, pledging 510 shares of General Motors common stock as collateral. The branch manager had Jimmy sign a Stock Power, a document allowing the bank to transfer ownership of the five stock certificates from Jimmy's name to the name of the bank should they need to liquidate the stock. Jimmy borrowed the banker's gold-plated A. T. Cross pen and signed five individual Stock Powers transferring negotiability to the bank. The branch manager put the stock certificates and signed Stock Powers in a sealed envelope, then placed the envelope in the branch vault to be held as collateral on the loan. Jimmy signed the loan agreement and agreed to have the $20,000 deposited to a newly opened Old Stone Bank checking account. Over the next three weeks, Jimmy withdrew $19,900 of the $20,000 deposit.

Ninety days passed, and Jimmy hadn't made any of the three monthly payments due on his $20,000 loan. The bank manager pulled the envelope holding 510 shares of GM. He stapled a Stock Power to each of the five stock certificates and had a messenger deliver the stock to the bank's Trust Department. On June 20, 1974 the Trust Department Trading Desk entered orders to sell 510 shares of General Motors at the market. The stock sold for $50.25 a share, generating $25,627.50. The branch manager was pleased, since it was more than enough to cover the $20,000 collateralized loan.

A week later, the Trust Department notified the branch manager that there was a problem with the sale of General Motors. When the Trust Department attempted to transfer the 510 shares to settle their trade, Chase Manhattan Bank refused to accept four certificates totaling 408 shares. Chase notified the Trust Department that four of the five stock certificates were worthless, since the Transfer Agent cancelled them after being reported as lost or stolen by the owner, James Maroni. The good news: one certificate for 102 shares, worth $5,125.50 was valid. Jimmy scammed the bank for more than $14,000.

Jimmy hired attorney Ray Kandle to defend him against felony charges of False Pretense and Theft by Deception. Kandle specialized in defending white-collar criminals, and Jimmy's case was ideal. Jimmy was a first-time offender with no prior record and while the dollar amount was substantial, there was no weapon involved and no physical violence. Ray Kandle respected his client's creativity. Bank robbery by stock certificate.

Kandle met with Assistant State Prosecutor Steve Murphy to work out a deal. The Prosecutor wanted restitution and jail time. Kandle told Murphy that Jimmy had pissed away the money on frequent trips to Miami, unsuccessful gambling and assorted non-prescription drugs. Kandle pleaded that none of the original $20,000 was left and Jimmy had no assets. The prosecutor wouldn't budge. They seemed to be at an impasse. Kandle proposed that he and Murphy meet with Judge Bob MacMillan. These men had a history of structuring fair deals in complicated cases without wasting the court's time. The defense attorney, prosecutor and judge worked well together, their relationship dating back to when all three were roommates at Providence College. As college kids, they listened to brilliant Dominican Fathers deliver eloquent homilies from the altar in PC's Aquinas Chapel. Now, twenty-five years later, as officers of the court, they filled their days listening to street thugs and white collar criminals lie under oath in Rhode Island Superior Court.

Kandle had Jimmy plead to one count of Theft by Deception and the False Pretense charge was dropped. Jimmy spent three months in the federal penitentiary at Fort Dix, got two years' probation and was ordered to undergo drug rehabilitation. Three months of Fed time was easy. Drug rehab was easier. Jimmy never smoked pot, did Quaaludes or any other drug for that matter. Confessing to drug use was merely a ruse to account for some of the missing money. Jimmy did his time, serving all 90 days, and came home in late November. His first night back, he treated himself to a dinner on Federal Hill. After pasta and chicken with capers, mushrooms and artichoke hearts, he went home and dug up three Autocrat coffee cans holding $15,000 in cash he had buried in his back yard.

Chapter 9

I entered the stately Court House Complex on the east bank
of the Providence River in the summer of '74, three months
after I was attacked. I was here to provide testimony to the
Grand Jury, testimony that would determine whether or
not Kohl would be indicted for what he had done to me.

As I entered the Grand Jury room, the door behind
me closed, separating me from my father and the detective
from Lincoln. I was alone, by myself, in a room of about
20 jurors and the prosecutor. The prosecutor introduced
me to the jurors and led me to a podium. I told my story
about how I had attended a meeting for my hockey team
and was hitchhiking home. I told them Kohl had picked
me up on Smithfield Avenue and I knew I was in trouble
when he refused to let me out of his car. I told them how
he drove through town, how I tried to jump from his car,
how he hit me and the route he took through town and

eventually to the dirt and gravel road off of Sherman Avenue. I told how I was pulled from the car with a belt around my neck, choking and on the verge of passing out, and how he beat, then raped me. I told how I memorized his license plate by reading it on the back of the inspection sticker on the windshield and how I tossed a chunk of cement against the hatchback window, shattering the glass, so I could prove to the cops I had been in that shitty little purple AMC Gremlin with the white stripe. I told about the agonizing run from his car to my house, and how I hid under a car and under hedges, hiding because I thought every car on the road was his and he was tracking me down and would kill me.

I was young and all alone, feeling scared, ashamed and vulnerable during my testimony, realizing the indictment of this evil bastard depended heavily on the strength of what I was saying. I was crying, shaking at times as I recalled, with vivid memories, the horrific events of that night. I remember looking up from the podium and seeing blue-haired old ladies openly crying as I told my story. In a few minutes, which seemed like an eternity, my testimony was over. The prosecutor thanked me and walked me out of the courtroom. I was shaking and crying, overcome with emotion and horrible memories of what Kohl had done to me. I remember hearing my father swear for the first time as he said, "Fuck that bastard; he's going to pay."

Months passed before I learned that a True Bill was returned, indicting Kohl on several charges. His judgment day was coming and the words I kept saying in my head as he beat and raped me would soon be true: "Stay alive tonight, and there's no way this son-of-a-bitch is going to get away with hurting me."

I spent the summer caddying at Kirkbrae Country Club on the north end of town. I'd ride my bike the six miles from Fairlawn to Kirkbrae, caddy 18 holes over four hours, then ride my bike six miles back home. It was a lot of work for a 14-year-old boy, but I was making $20 to $25 a day in cash and it was worth it.

I enjoyed caddying and being around successful, powerful businessmen, doctors, lawyers and judges. Spending four hours on the golf course, walking with these guys, hearing them bullshit with each other, helping them find lost balls and dropping new ones when they didn't, was an enjoyable way for a kid to spend the summer. If you were a good caddy, the members would tip the Caddy Master and pass on a good word. If the Caddy Master got tipped and praise, he'd be sure to send you out with good golfers and big tippers the next day. Over time, members got to know you and if you were any good, they'd request you by name. I was good and there were a few men that I caddied for regularly, one being Ray Kandle.

Mr. Kandle was a well-known, well-respected criminal defense attorney with a client list that included mostly white-collar criminals facing federal charges and men with alleged ties to organized crime. I went to school with his niece, had met him at her birthday parties and he was a very good friend of my Uncle Mike, The Syrian. He'd ask for me by name and I caddied for him almost every Saturday, teeing off before 7:40 a.m. and finishing before noon. He'd buy me a snack and a coffee milk when we made the turn after the ninth hole and I'd be home before one o'clock with $25 dollars in my pocket before most of my friends had gotten out of bed.

One weekend, the other guys in the foursome were teasing Mr. Kandle about an article in the Providence Journal about some of his clients. The article stated that several men had been arrested for breaking into the National Guard Armory in Lincoln and stealing weapons. The Journal reported that their attorney, Ray Kandle, had no comment. I remember one of his golf partners teasing, "Hey Ray, what can you say about men who break into a National Guard Armory to steal weapons? They're not your average, everyday burglars."

Mr. Kandle was very kind to me. He took a sincere interest in me, asking me how I was doing, what I wanted to do when I grew up, where I wanted to go to college, what I was doing to have fun during the summer. He asked me about the Boston Red Sox, which I knew nothing about, and my opinion about which way his putt would break. I really enjoyed caddying for him.

Although I didn't know it at the time, one of the most powerful criminal attorneys in Rhode Island knew what Kohl had done to me, knew about his porn business, knew about Kohl's previous arrests and prison time. He knew Kohl had been indicted for what he had done to me before anyone outside of the courthouse knew. He knew it all. My Uncle Mike and Mr. Kandle were close friends. They shared mutual clients. When Uncle Mike went to Mr. Kandle and told him what happened, Kandle offered to keep an eye on me and to look into Ronald Kohl. At the age of 14, I was being protected by one of the most powerful, most respected, most feared, most connected attorneys in New England, a man who had bullet wounds from being shot and always shot under 90.

My summer morning bike rides to Kirkbrae were beautiful. I'd get up around 6 a.m. and watch the sun rise as I rode to the club. The ride up Smithfield Avenue got more beautiful the farther I rode. My first sight as daylight broke was the dam and waterfall at Barney's Pond. Then I'd see great houses on Great Road, bicycling past the past, like the Eleazer Arnold House, built in 1693, and the Israel Arnold house, built in 1720. I'd pedal past the Moffit Mill and Hearthside, the only house I knew that had a name, both built in 1810, then ride by the Mowry Tavern, built in 1820. I'd head north up Great Road after passing the open fields of Chase & Butterfly Farm, with its giant American Flag draped between two grain silos. If you're riding a bike, you notice that this section of Great Road is a very long, barely discernible, ever-so-slightly rising incline, starting at the Farm, going past Day 'N Night Golf Course, past the cattle field and the horse stables, and ending three miles later, where this great road meets Washington Highway. It was a beautiful uphill pedal in the morning for anyone with their eyes open and an effortless, fun-filled, three mile sit-back-and-don't-bother-to-pedal downhill coast on the way home.

There were many afternoons when I would stop at the Chase and Butterfly Farm after spending the morning caddying, put my bike down in the field and take a nap. As the summer wore on, I was feeling increasingly tired, day after day. There were many days when the early afternoon catnaps in the field were a necessity, because I was too tired to continue the ride home. It was a wonderful, Norman Rockwellian way to take a break and get some rest as I fell asleep facing the grain silos and that big, beautiful, oversized American Flag.

In September 1974, one day before I was to enter my sophomore year at Lincoln High School, I was admitted to the Memorial Hospital in Pawtucket. I was about to learn why I had been feeling so tired during the summer.

I had been spending the summer doing things 14 year old kids did in Lincoln: fishing in Spec's Pond, caddying, bowling, playing baseball, basketball, boxing at the Boy's Club and hanging out with my friends. I became severely bruised that summer, literally from my ankles to my wrists, with huge bruises on my legs, thighs, upper arms and ribs. I thought nothing of it, being an active kid and relatively small for my age. The bruises didn't concern me. Although they were big, they didn't hurt.

I had a physical in late August, and my routine blood work came back showing a platelet count of 3,000. A normal platelet count for a healthy person is approximately 300,000. Platelets are the cells in your blood that create blood clots when you bleed. With dangerously low platelets, any trauma, simple trauma like falling down, bumping your head or getting checked in a hockey game could cause uncontrollable, fatal, internal bleeding and stroke. The bruises that didn't concern me because they didn't hurt weren't bruises caused by being hit or bumped. They were spontaneous hemorrhages, internal bleeding pooling under my skin. With just 3,000 platelets, I was missing 99 percent of my clotting factor.

I spent the next two months in and out of the hospital, with doctors ruling out cancer, leukemia and lymphoma, and undergoing surgeries to remove my spleen and some lymph nodes. I was finally diagnosed with Idiopathic Thrombocytopenic Purpura, ITP for short. I celebrated my 15th birthday in a private room in the pediatric intensive care unit with family, a few friends, a birthday cake and a few nurses singing "Happy Birthday." It was here, in Memorial Hospital as a young ITP patient, that I met a remarkable man, a man who left his mark on me with his brilliance, his professionalism, his stature, his presence, his knowledge, his experience, his compassion, his manner, his carriage, his humor, his caring, his tolerance, his wit, his intellect, his *joie de vivre*. Early 60s, 6 foot 2, 200 pounds, a full head of swept-back gray hair, a real prince, a bloodline descendant of Italian royalty. Dr. Mario Giovanni Baldini, Chief of Staff and Director of Oncology at Memorial Hospital. One of the Men in My Town.

Dr. Baldini explained to me that blood platelets are produced in my body's bone marrow. ITP is a common secondary condition for cancer patients, with their ITP being caused by chemotherapy destroying their marrow's ability to produce platelets. Unlike cancer patients, my bone marrow is healthy and produces platelets. My ITP is caused by a defect in my body which causes my immune system to recognize my platelets as foreign and destroy them. It's rare that ITP is chronic. As luck would have it, I have a rare case of chronic, lifelong ITP.

At first, I had symptoms whenever my platelet count started to drop: bruise-like hemorrhages, tiny spots of blood around my ankles and nosebleeds. Over time, the symptoms stopped appearing, even when my platelets reached dangerously low levels, which could result in spontaneous, uncontrollable bleeding. Frequent blood tests, sometimes weekly, helped me monitor my platelet count and could foretell when treatment was necessary. But there were several occasions when my count dropped rapidly, from apparently safe levels to dangerous, life-threatening levels, seemingly overnight, with no warning, no symptoms, silently and deadly. When my platelet count dropped to 6,000 or so, which it did periodically, I ran the risk of a spontaneous brain hemorrhage.

Between frequent visits to the Police Department, the Court House, doctor's offices and the hospital, 1974 was gone and so was my youth, my innocence, my trust, my childhood, stolen away by two total strangers that snuck up on me unexpectedly, attacking without warning: Ronald Thomas Kohl and ITP. Fortunately for me, whether I was home in bed or in a hospital bed, there were men in my town taking care of me, looking out for me, keeping me safe, and helping me stay alive.

I learned more in that summer than most people learn in a lifetime. Kohl and ITP both threatened to kill me, yet ironically, they gave me a new appreciation of life. They forced me to come face-to-face with my own mortality, to consider death and realize the fragility of life. They gave me reason to reflect on what's important to me, what life's about, what I'm supposed to be, supposed to do, what's meaningful, what's insignificant, what's irrelevant, what's mundane, what's magnificent, how I live, how I love, what I believe, what I abhor, what I stand for, what I want to do, should do and how I want to be remembered. Deep thoughts for a 15 year old kid and great revelations no matter how old you are.

Chapter 10

I thought it was a secret, my shameful secret, with just a few people having been told about what Kohl had done to me. Years later I learned that a group of men in my town knew. They knew what Kohl had done to me, what he looked like, where he lived, where he had lived in the past, where he worked, where he hung out, what he drove, where he bought gas, where he shopped for groceries, where his car was parked at night. They knew the credit card number on his Shell gas card, what time he left his house in the morning, the route he always drove to work and that he never went out for lunch because he packed his own. They knew his landlord's name and how much he paid in rent. They had the account numbers of his Citizens Bank checking account and his VISA card. They had his signature from carbon copies of charge card receipts and they had pictures of him, his house, his business and his car. What they knew they kept to themselves. What they knew kept me and every kid in the neighborhood safe. What they knew would be useful when the time was right, or when they were told Kohl's time was up.

More than a year had passed since Kohl raped me, and I was concerned about not having gone to trial. What were the cops doing? What was Kohl doing? He was arrested and indicted, and yet we still hadn't gone to trial. What was going on?

Trials had been scheduled, and then postponed several times over the past year. The prosecutor would tell us we were going to trial and I would become anxious about having to tell my story again, reliving the horror of March 1, 1974 as Kohl's attorney tried to keep his scumbag client out of prison. I was looking forward to facing down Kohl, telling a judge and jury that this man beat and raped me. I was looking forward to having the courage to say in open court, "This is the guy," so he'd be put away and wouldn't be free to do it again, wouldn't be able to beat and rape another child, a child that might not be as lucky as I was, a child that might not be able to stay alive through an attack by this serial predator pedophile. But the trial date kept being pushed forward, another month or two, again and again, and in the meantime, Kohl was free on bail, cruising for boys on the quiet streets of Cumberland, Central Falls, Lincoln, Pawtucket and North Providence.

Ron Kohl was free on bail, but he wasn't a free man. He could rarely go out in public without being conspicuously followed. The Feds were blatant in their pursuit of Kohl, and for obvious reasons. They wanted everyone to know, everywhere he went, that federal agents were following this guy. When he stopped at McGee's Restaurant on Dexter Street for a coffee, the Feds went in and ordered black coffee to go. When he went to get a haircut, the Feds parked their unmarked Plymouth Fury cruiser outside the barbershop. When he drove into Providence to pick up copies of *Hustler, Oui, Gallery, Genesis, Screw* and *Club* from his distributor, the Feds hung around just long enough to be seen by the guys loading the magazines into Kohl's car. The constant presence of the Feds drew the attention of Kohl's business partners, and it wasn't long before the guys providing magazines, pictures, films and financing were having him followed. He knew the Feds were watching him, suspected his business partners were watching him, but had no clue he was being watched by the men in my town and the guys they knew. Another thing Kohl didn't know: for over a year, the Feds kept getting his trial date postponed so they could have more time to pressure him to roll over on his contacts in the booming pornography business.

Kohl was feeling the pressure. He was an indicted recidivist, facing another trial for sex crimes, and didn't want to go back to prison. The Feds were squeezing him every day, following him and making it uncomfortable for customers to go into his store. He suspected the Feds had something to do with Dexter Credit Union turning him down for a loan and the recent visit from the Providence office of the IRS. As difficult as it was, time on the street, even with the Feds on his tail, was better than time in prison. Kohl knew if he cooperated with the Feds and rolled on his partners, he could cut a deal on the beating and rape charges out of Lincoln, but he'd be a dead man. If he didn't cooperate, the Feds would make his life miserable, his business would continue to suffer and his partners would think he was skimming.

By the summer of '75, the guys from Providence and New York were growing increasingly wary of the attention Kohl was getting from the Feds. Would he flip? Was he a snitch? Kohl hated the Feds for what they were doing to him. More than ever, he wanted to strike out against them, a reaction they were looking to provoke so they could lock him up. Kohl felt taunted and provoked by the constant presence of the Feds, watching his every move and photographing him, his customers and his store. Kohl was growing increasingly agitated, feeling manipulated, powerless, helpless. His life and his choices were no longer his; they were no longer in his control. But what choice did he have? Cooperating or not cooperating with the Feds could be lethal. When the pressure got to be too much, Kohl sought refuge in his old habits, bad habits. He was back on the street, seeking to regain his lost sense of power, domination and control. He was out hunting for young boys again.

He was filled with anger as he woke to the early morning sunlight breaking through the single window in his tiny bedroom. It was going to be a beautiful, bright, sunny day in Central Falls, but not in the dark world that consumed Ronald Kohl. Before his feet hit the floor, he started his day with a silent thought running through his head. *Cops. Assholes. What bullshit do they have in store for me today?*

He shaved his face, meticulously removing the night's stubble. Upward strokes with a straight edge razor, then downward strokes over the same area, followed by horizontal strokes, left to right, then right to left. Rinse and then do it again. Up, down, horizontal, removing every hair, every bit of stubble. It was a slow and tedious shave but the result was worth it. He peered into the bathroom mirror, inspecting himself, admiring himself. He gazed at the skin on his cheekbones just below the eyes and his jaw line from his ear to his chin. He ran the index and middle fingers of his left hand over his face. The smell of Johnson & Johnson baby powder filled the bathroom. He was pleased with what he saw, what he felt. Baby smooth skin. He was perfect.

He slipped into his blue double-knit polyester boot-cut Haggar slacks, white shirt, white patent leather belt and black ankle boots. He reached up to the top shelf in his bedroom closet for the empty backpack. It was time to go shopping for the things he needed to go hunting for his next victim.

He walked to Broad Street to catch the Number 71 Bus to the store. He was full of himself, knowing what he was about to do, outsmarting the cops who were watching his car down the block, not watching his house. "I'm smarter than they are," he said to himself as he walked away from his apartment and muttered, "Stupid fuckin' cops," as he stepped into the bus.

Eighteen minutes later he was walking into Ann & Hope. He knew exactly what he needed to buy: one pair of Converse All Star Chuck Taylor leather high tops, Alberto VO5 Hairspray, a size 50 belt from the Big & Tall section in men's clothing, and duct tape. The "Chucks" would be his lure in his newly-concocted, lurid plan. It was a perfect plan, and this time he wouldn't get caught.

Kohl went looking for boys at the outdoor basketball courts where Higginson meets Lonsdale Avenue in Central Falls and the courts behind the Club Paradise on Reservoir Avenue in Lincoln. He hung out at the courts, leaning against his car, taking pictures of shirtless young boys playing three-on-three basketball. He came here night after night, following the same routine, making himself inconspicuous–a plain-vanilla, nothing of a man, blending in with the scenery. An unimportant, insignificant nobody, not worthy of being noticed. He took pictures, a dozen or so every time, hundreds over a few weeks, of shirtless, sweaty teenage boys breathing heavily, pushing and shoving, rough housing, horsing around while they played b-ball. And while he was there, all he was focusing on was singling out the one he'd approach, the weakest of the herd, the lonely one, the one boy that didn't quite fit in, the one boy all the other boys teased. He was willing to wait days, weeks if he had to, before making his move. He had a plan and knew he had made mistakes in the past when he wasn't deliberate, when his urges forced him to act spontaneously. *Be patient*, he thought. *Take your time, stick to the plan. It will be worth the wait and this time, you won't get caught.*

Kohl closed his eyes and ran through the plan over and over in his head. When he identified his mark and the time was right, he'd strike up a conversation about how he happened to have a brand new pair of Chuck Taylor All Stars, still in the box, size 9, that were too small for him but maybe the kid would like them. Getting a kid to take a look at a brand new pair of Chucks would be easy. Buying new shoes, jewelry, jeans, men's suits, even small electronics like CB radios and cassette decks out of a car trunk was a common small business practice in my town—deep discount mobile retail on wheels.

Once he had him near the car, he'd spray Alberto VO5 hairspray in the kid's eyes, temporarily blinding him. Three pre-cut strips of duct tape would be on the car dashboard. The larger one, to be used first, would go over the kid's mouth to silence him. The two smaller strips of tape would go over his eyes. Duct tape the kid's wrists, one over the other, so he couldn't fight back. Loop the extra-long size 50 belt over the kid's head to keep him under control then drive to a secluded spot in the woods. Leave the boy in the woods, bound, beaten and naked, eyes covered with duct tape. If he can't see anything, he can't tell the cops what he saw. With his eyes still closed, Kohl smiled. His plan was perfect. The only thing he needed now was a boy.

Chapter 11

I was riding my bike on Smithfield Avenue on a sunny summer afternoon in the first week of June. Minding my own business, riding around looking for my friends, when out of nowhere, son-of-a-bitch, Kohl's car passed me on the avenue, just in front of Cumberland Farms. It was definitely him, in the light of day, the white stripe on the purple AMC Gremlin, the memorized license plate clearly visible. The bastard had gotten within 20 feet of me, without me knowing he was even there. My heart was racing, fear filled my body, thoughts raced through my head. Did he know where I lived? Was he here looking for me? Did he see me as he drove by? What was he doing here?

I turned my bike around and went in the other direction. If he was looking for me, he'd have to turn his car around to come after me. If I could get behind the auto body, I could cut through the fence to the playground on

Cecile Street and could be home in a few minutes. Or I could just go to Dennis for help.

Dennis owned a tailor shop on the corner of Smithfield and Reservoir Avenue. If I could get past Cumberland Farms and cut behind Sportsman's bar, I could get to his shop. Three minutes after seeing Kohl on Smithfield Avenue, I was off my bike and safe inside of Giordano Tailors.

I dropped my bike outside and ran in. Dennis excused himself from a customer and took me by the arm. He knew something was terribly wrong and without asking a question or saying a thing, he walked me behind the counter, past his cash register and pulled aside the fabric curtain separating the front of his shop from the cutting and sewing room. There, behind the curtain, sat two men at a table with three handguns in plain sight. One man put his index finger up over his lips, signaling me to be quiet. Dennis sat me down, told me these guys were his friends and that he'd be back in a minute. The fabric curtain swept aside again and Dennis was gone, back to the front of his shop to take care of his customer. One 15-year-old boy, two grown men smoking cigars and three handguns. We sat in silence, waiting for Dennis to return.

I didn't know if the guns belonged to the two guys and Dennis or if the guys were buying guns or selling guns. It didn't matter. I was scared because Kohl was on Smithfield Avenue, maybe looking for me, and I now felt safe, very safe and protected, in the presence of Dennis, his two friends and their three revolvers.

Dennis came back behind the curtain and took me outside. We sat in his Lincoln Continental Mark III and I told him what happened. He asked me if I was sure it was Kohl. He told me to take my time and think through exactly what I saw and to tell him if there was any chance it might not have been him. I told Dennis that I was positive, that I'd never forget the car, it was purple, for Christ's sake, and I read the rear license plate as the car passed me on my left: It was him. I was positive.

Dennis took me back into the shop and told his friends he was locking up and would be back in a few minutes. He picked my bike up off the sidewalk and put it in his store. He put up the "closed" sign, locked the front door and told me to get in his car. He drove down Smithfield Avenue and through several blocks around my house. We didn't see Kohl, and he told me that he'd be keeping an eye out for him over the next few days. Dennis reached over, rubbed the top of my head, told me to get out of his car and to come by his shop tomorrow to get my bike. As I got out of his Continental, he powered down the driver's side window and called me back to his car. "It's going to be o.k., bambino," he said. "We're going to take care of this."

The siren on the roof of the Fairlawn-Lincoln Fire Department blared its call, piercing the silence of an early, beautiful, sunny weekday morning. Volunteer firefighters made up of local businessmen, retired men, high school seniors, college kids, off-duty cops and night shift guys home from work ran or drove the few blocks they needed to go to get to the fire station. Dennis put down his morning

coffee, locked the front door to his tailor shop and drove
two-tenths of a mile to the station. The owner of the Amoco
gas station was already behind the wheel of the 1959 Ward
LaFrance pumper, so Dennis pulled his gear from the rack,
got on the back step of the pumper and strapped himself in.
As the truck pulled out from the bay, one of the local kids,
a 19 year old sophomore at Providence College, ran into the
station, grabbed his gear from the hooks on the wall and
jumped on the rear step of the pumper as it pulled out of
the station and onto Smithfield Avenue.

With three men on the pumper, it went south on Smithfield Avenue, by Dennis's locked shop, took a right onto
Weeden Street and raced up Cobble Hill Road. The truck
could have made this trip by itself, since the firemen typi-
cally made this run a dozen or so times during the fall to
respond to brush fires at Smart's field. But today was different. The pumper was racing up Cobble Hill, with only the
driver having access to the radio, which blared a warning
from the Lincoln Police dispatcher, "Two story, multi-fam-
ily dwelling, visible smoke and flames. Mutual Aid call,
Saylesville and Lime Rock will respond." This wasn't going
to be another walk in Smart's field with a five gallon Indian
Back Pack fire pump.

As the fire truck arrived first on scene, the driver took
responsibility for the pump, the college kid took responsibility for dragging 100 feet of hose to the closest fire
hydrant and Dennis grabbed a Scott Air Pack from the side
cabinet of the pumper. Throwing the Scott Air Pack on
his back, he put the air mask over his face, put on his hel-
met and turned on the air. As he was gearing up, a second

truck arrived on scene from Saylesville, a section of town just north of Fairlawn. Dennis felt a tap on his shoulder as a fireman from Saylesville came up by his side. The masked fireman grabbed hold of Dennis' Air Pack waist belt and snapped the male end of Dennis's belt to the female end of his own waist belt. The two men, now connected by five feet of nylon belt, entered the front door of the burning house to look for bodies.

Dennis and the fireman from Saylesville began the slow process of carefully walking up the center stairway colonial. The house, originally built in the mid 1800s, had been renovated and converted into two downstairs apartments and two upstairs apartments. With flames shooting out of the roofline from the second floor at the rear of the building, they knew exactly where they had to go. But before they got there, their job was to look for people who needed help, or people who were unconscious, overcome by smoke and lying in the hall or on the stairs.

The smoke was so thick and black that Dennis literally lost sight of the other fireman within seconds of entering the house. Although they couldn't see each other, they were connected by the waist belts of their Air Packs and by an unspoken bond between firemen. The five foot strap served two purposes. They couldn't get separated and if either one fell, the other would help. No one gets left behind.

Checking the first floor doors for heat and finding none, they began walking up the center stairway, dragging their feet across each step, into the riser and across the next step. Dragging their feet, never lifting them off the floor, to be sure the steps below them hadn't been burned out and to be sure they didn't step over the outstretched hand, arm, leg or body of an adult or a child, lying unconscious on the steps.

Dennis followed the fireman from Saylesville, step by step, through the pitch–black, blinding smoke in zero visibility. Unable to see, both firemen were feeling their way up the stairs, with their right arms stretched out, their right hands touching the wall, guiding them up the curved staircase, 16 steps in all, to the landing on the second floor. A few feet down the short hallway put the firemen between the door to the apartment at the front of the house and the door to the apartment that was burning in the rear. The fireman from Saylesville used his Hooligan Tool to pry open the door to the apartment that wasn't on fire and led Dennis in. They quickly searched for people, dragging their feet, flipping over beds, and opening closets. In less than two minutes they were back in the hallway and again used the Hooligan to pop open the door to the apartment on fire.

With one fireman on each side of the doorway, both bent forward slightly to look into the apartment as the door popped opened. It was fully engulfed, with flames filling the apartment. Dennis imagined that this was what Hell must look like. Then, in a flash, a line of fire raced across the kitchen floor, through the entry, out the door of the apartment and into the hall. The line of fire moved between the two firemen, up the hallway wall, and danced across the ceiling above their heads. As both firemen held their positions in the hall, one on each side of the apartment doorway, the fire licked the ceiling circling above their heads, alive in its very real threat of death. Then, as quickly as it appeared from inside of the apartment, it retreated from the ceiling, down the hallway wall, and crawled again between Dennis and the other fireman and back into the apartment.

The apartment was full of flames and the temperature in the apartment was approaching 1,000 degrees. If anyone was in there, it was too late. The fireman from Saylesville who led the way in and up the stairs yelled through his Scott Air Pack mask, "It's time to go." Dennis turned around and led the way down the stairs, arm outstretched, left hand on the wall for guidance, dragging his feet, step by step, 16 steps to go. Halfway down the stairs, with the smoke still thick and no visibility, he crashed into Chris Galligan as Chris was coming up the stairs with a hose. Dennis screamed to Chris that they didn't find anyone in the house and placed his left foot against the hose. As Chris continued up the stairs, Dennis used the hose as his guide to lead the way out of the burning house. As he continued down the steps, he saw a tiny amount of light, sunlight, coming in through the door at the bottom of the stairs. With each step the smoke was less intense and the sunlight illuminated the doorway. If Hell looked like the room at the top of the stairs, Dennis wondered if the glimmer of light, growing brighter as he took each step toward the front door, was like the light people saw when they passed to Heaven.

As he approached the front door, the bell on his Air Pack began to ring, signaling Dennis and everyone who could hear it that his air tank was running out of air. A few more steps, and Dennis led himself and the fireman from Saylesville out of the building.

EMTs pulled the buckle on the Scott Air Pack waist straps, separating Dennis and the other fireman before they were taken to separate ambulances and given oxygen.

Over the next several hours, twenty firemen would fight the blaze before the house eventually collapsed and burned to the ground. As hours passed, Dennis tormented himself, questioning if he left someone behind. Did he fail to find someone who was trapped in the house? Did he fail to help someone who needed his help? Did someone die today because he wasn't able to get into the burning apartment? Fortunately, the police were able to locate every resident. No one was in the house as it burned and collapsed. No one was there as Dennis and the other volunteer fireman bravely entered the burning house, without water, with one objective, to do what they were trained to do: to go in and save a life.

Dennis the tailor locked his shop that morning and strapped a Scott Air Pack on his back to enter a burning house looking for bodies, putting his life at risk to save people he didn't know, total strangers. This brave man who would walk into a burning building in a life–offering, unselfish act of bravery and kindness, was as comfortable with a Scott Air Pack strapped on his back as he was with a snub-nosed Smith & Wesson .38 strapped to the inside of his left ankle.

Random acts of bravery and kindness to the innocent came as easy as calculated acts of ruthless violence against the guilty when you dealt with the men in my town.

Chapter 12

Bobby lived alone on the third floor of the dilapidated tenement on the corner of Weeden Street, across from two bars, a gas station and a pharmacy. When he wasn't drinking in one bar, he was betting in the other. When he wasn't bullshitting with the kid pumping gas at the Getty station, he was shoplifting Fannie Farmer chocolates from the pharmacy and selling them for petty cash. He was a harmless, unemployed part-time criminal and full-time gambler. The problem for Bobby was he'd bet that the sun would shine tomorrow morning without checking the weather forecast first.

He lived in a three-room apartment. Bedroom, kitchen, bath. Three rooms if you count the bath. He owned a bed, a lamp made out of a Gallo wine bottle, a lawn chair, an A.M. radio, a frying pan and a black and white TV. He loved his place. The $35 weekly rent was right and it was on the bus line to Lincoln Downs. He could take the RIPTA bus up Cobble Hill and in six minutes and two miles be at the track to bet on the ponies. Today he was working on covering rent. He was two weeks late and ran the chance of finding the six things he owned in the street if he didn't pay up within the next few days. He had $26 left from his unemployment and workman's comp as he walked into the bar while he pretended to wait for the bus. He sat next to the oldest drunk in the bar. Bobby ordered a glass of Narragansett as he lifted a few singles from the pile of bills in front of the old man and paid 50 cents for the 35 cent glass of beer. He had been caught doing this before and got his ass kicked, but the unsuspecting old man had been drinking for hours and didn't notice. He shot the glass of beer and moved to the door with three dollars and 50 cents more than he had five minutes ago. $3.50. Not quite enough for two $2 bets.

The track was full of the usual miscreants: the down-on-their-luck crowd, the unemployed, the desperate looking to hit a long shot, the hopeful looking to get lucky with a bet or with one of the lonely women who hung out here, hoping to hook up with a winner. There were the hustlers, hookers and petty thieves that would lift your purse. There were mobsters and mobster wannabes. There were college kids and housewives and guys who should have been at work. There were professional gamblers who knew the track, the horses, the jockeys, the grooms and their families. There were people betting that didn't know shit, didn't know a thoroughbred from a trotter, didn't know a trifecta box from a box of Triscuits. There were the regular drunks, sloppy drunks, and violent drunks betting on horses that were thoroughbreds in name only. Lincoln Downs wasn't Churchill Downs. Lincoln was a mile-plus oval dirt left-handed track, six miles north of downtown Providence, running $2,000 claimers. The best it had to offer was the opportunity to watch Mike Lapensee and Denise Boudrot ride. Denise was one of the few woman jockeys in the game and her success on less successful horses earned her the nickname Long Shot Lady. Bobby loved Denise. They had never met and never would, but the way she rode horses made him money. Who said you can't buy love?

Bobby was luckless in the first three races, losing $18.00. He had eleven bucks left and decided to skip the fourth and fifth. The sixth offered some hope. Denise was riding.

The board showed nine horses running in the sixth. He let the clock tick down to post-time as the odds changed as bets were made. With two minutes to post, the favorite was going off at 2-1 and the longest shot was a dog masquerading as a horse paying 189-1. Bobby liked the idea of turning a $2 bet into $378 but he had a rule. If Denise was riding, he bet her horse, and this afternoon she was standing in the irons of Precious Dancer, a 67-1 long shot with another opportunity to earn her nickname. He walked up to the window and bet $2 to win on Precious Dancer. He was feeling lucky at this very minute, so he bet a $2 Exacta on Precious Dancer and the 2-1 favorite, Crown Challenger.

Crown Challenger broke from the gate at the bell, taking firm command of the lead. Precious Dancer dueled with her for the first quarter mile before dropping back to third, allowing Crown Challenger to lead the field most of the way. At the top of the stretch, Crown Challenger opened up a two and a half length lead and looked to be home free before Precious Dancer switched leads and Denise made a bold, strong move out three wide, taking over the lead position inside the 1/8 pole. Denise held the lead to the finish, with Crown Challenger half a length back in second.

In a little less than two minutes, Bobby's $2 to win on Denise paid $136.20. His $2 Exacta on Denise and the favorite, Crown Challenger paid $605.20. It was time to pay the rent.

With $748.90 in his pocket, Bobby took a cab home. It was the luckiest day in his life and the most he ever won. He was on top of the world. Invincible. Ghetto rich. He had a feeling that his life would never be the same. He was right. But he had no way of knowing exactly how bad it was going to get.

Chapter 13

Some people shouldn't bet. Bobby blew through the $741.40 he won in just a few days. He paid his past due rent and the next two months in advance, not because it was the prudent thing to do to be sure he had a place to live, but because his landlord was going to throw his ass out if he didn't. He hitched a ride down Lonsdale Avenue to Ann & Hope and bought himself new Pumas, a Timex watch and a new pair of Wrangler jeans. He bought a quarter-ounce bag of pot and a new bong. He spent hours at Sportsman's, on the corner of Reservoir and Smithfield Avenue, drinking glasses of beer with Jack Daniels chasers. He went back to the track, bet heavily and lost often. Ghetto rich to shit-house broke in 4 days: not a new story for Bobby. He had good luck, bad luck and no luck, but he always seemed to get by. He had money at the beginning of the week, was out of money by the end of the week and it was never a problem. He'd bet and win again. It's how he lived.

June 11, 1975. The Boston Red Sox are playing the Chicago White Sox, in Chicago. Rhode Island doesn't have a major league baseball team, so like most sports fans in New England, everyone in Rhode Island adopted the Red Sox, the Bruins and the Patriots as their hometown teams. Bobby needed some quick cash, so he did something he knew was foolish. He bet big on Chicago, figuring the White Sox would have the hometown advantage.

Betting on Chicago to win wasn't foolish. Betting when he was broke wasn't the smartest thing to do, but it wasn't foolish. Foolish was tripling up, betting $75 on Chicago to beat Boston with three different bookies, one in Pawtucket, one in Lincoln, and The Syrian in Central Falls. Bobbie split his bets because no one bookie would give him more than $100 credit and if he won, which he was sure he would, it wouldn't matter.

Bobbie had a feeling, a feeling his life was about to change. He was right.

With 5,228 in attendance at Comiskey Park, Boston and Chicago began playing what would no doubt be one of the year's most memorable games. Bobby was drinking beer, watching the game at Sportsman's, working up a sweat as the game entered the bottom of the ninth, tied 7-7. One run, either way, would pay or cost him $225–$225 he could use, $225 he didn't have to lose. He was a gambler, hoping the run would fall in his favor and the

$225 would fall into his pocket. Chicago closed out the bottom of the ninth scoreless. Would this game ever end? It was time to go home. He'd spent the last few hours drinking beer in Sportsman's, half-heartedly cheering for Boston, silently hoping they'd lose, and now he was out of beer money.

Bobby opened one of three cans of Narragansett beer in his refrigerator while Chicago fans at Comiskey Park popped open cold cans of Pabst Blue Ribbon. He turned on his Gallo wine bottle lamp, sat his sad ass in his lawn chair in his dingy little third floor apartment and turned on his AM radio to listen to the rest of the game. The 10th inning came and went. The 11th, 12th, 13th innings were scoreless. Boston and Chicago had battled for almost four hours, and neither side could break the 7-7 tie. The tension was tearing Bobby apart.

At the top of the 14th inning, Rich "Goose" Gossage, pitching for Chicago, was facing Cecile Cooper, pinch-hitting for Doug Griffin. Cooper hit a ground ball to Gossage for the easy flip to Tony Muser at first base for the first out. One out, two to go.

Bobby's praying Boston will go down on the next two batters and put an end to his four-hour torture. Bernie Carbo, Boston's left fielder, is at the plate. He's hit by a pitch and takes first base. With Carbo on first, Rick Burleson, the short stop, pops out to Bob Coluccio in right field, as Carbo steals second base. Two outs, one to go, with Bernie Carbo on second. Things are looking good. Bobby is hopeful.

Burleson high-fives Carl Yastrzemski as they pass each other and Yaz walks up to the plate. Yastrzemski, in a moment that's revered by Boston fans, breaks the 7-7 tie with a home run in the top of the 14th inning, bringing Bernie Carbo home and giving Boston a two-run lead over Chicago, 9-7.

Bobby's apoplectic as he throws his half empty can of Narragansett against his windowless wall. He suddenly feels nauseous. In an anti-climatic moment, batting after Yastrzemski's homerun, Fred Lynn strikes out, closing the inning for Boston and bringing Chicago in from the field for their turn at bat.

At the bottom of the 14th, Boston pulls pitcher Roger Moret and trots out Diego Segui to the mound. Chicago's second baseman, Jorge Orta, draws four balls from Segui and gets a walk to first. Catcher Brian Downing hits an infield ground ball, getting to first, while Orta is forced out at second. Bob Coluccio hits a clean single, advancing Downing to second base. With one out and men on first and second, Bobby now has reason to be hopeful. While his Gallo wine bottle lamp is throwing off shadows from a dim 60 watt bulb, things are looking brighter. Then, with just a few pitches, Boston's Segui puts down two batters, as Bucky Dent hits a fly ball to left field and Carlos May hits a line drive to Bob Heise at second base.

Game over. Boston 9, Chicago 7 in four hours and eight minutes. The longest game of the season came to an end as Bobby sat in his lawn chair, owing $225 he didn't have after the longest game of his life.

Chapter 14

Bobby was in trouble–$225 was a king's ransom. He settled with his bookie once a week and with no cash and no way to earn an honest buck, he was looking for ways to avoid having to hide until he could cash next month's unemployment check.

There had to be a way. Bobby was hanging out on Smithfield Avenue, walking back and forth to the four bars on the three blocks between Reservoir Avenue and Weeden Street. Kevin came out of Club Paradise with a mid-afternoon buzz and started bullshitting with Bobby. Bobby, desperate for cash, came right out and asked if Kevin had anything going on where he might need some help, because Bobby was looking for an opportunity to earn.

Kevin and Bobby go way back. There's history between these two guys and their families, good history. They grew up in the same tenement, Kevin's family on the first floor,

Bobby's on the second. They went to school together since kindergarten, but graduated in different years because Bobby had to repeat a grade every so often.

When they were growing up as young boys, Bobby's father owned a bakery and when Kevin's mom couldn't afford to put food on the table, Bobby's father made sure she and her boys had something to eat. No questions asked, no promises made, no payment expected, no quid pro quo. It was just one good man doing a very kind thing for his downstairs neighbor and her kids. When he was older, Kevin's mom told him what Bobby's dad had done and ever since then, Kevin kept an eye on Bobby, just because.

Fortunately for Bobby, Kevin did have something going on and could use some help. Kevin had plans to unload a truck parked at the loading dock on the Industrial Circle. Sounds simple enough, except they'd have to do it at night, in the dark, because it wasn't their truck. Breaking into tractor trailers parked at the loading dock was just another way Kevin made a buck, and it was time to see what was in the back of an out-of-state 18-wheeler.

Kevin went to his brother's auto body after closing and pulled license plates off a black 1971 Cadillac Fleetwood 66 Brougham. He screwed them onto the bumper of a Ford Econoline van that was in for bodywork and threw a flashlight, two pair of gloves, wire cutters and a police radio from Radio Shack onto the passenger seat. He drove down Smithfield Avenue to pick up Bobby. He told Bobby what he had planned as they continued down Smithfield Avenue, took a right onto Gardiner Avenue and parked the van at the end of the street. As they walked down Industrial Circle, both guys were breaking a sweat. No matter how many times they pulled shit like this, it still elevated their pulses and got their adrenaline pumping.

Kevin cut the chain link fence at a fence post and slid the fencing to the right. Bobby bent forward at the waist and with a raised left arm sweeping from his right shoulder down across his chest and past his left hip said, "After you." Kevin walked through the fence and toward the rear of the loading dock where seven trailers sat silent and alone in the dark. Kevin decided to hit the fourth trailer just because it was in the middle. During the ride to Gardiner Avenue, Kevin told Bobby that it was important to remain silent while they worked the trailer so they could hear sounds of cars coming through the yard, people talking, footsteps or dogs.

The trailer wasn't locked but it did have a shipping seal that had to be broken in order to open the rear door. Seals are applied by shippers at the beginning of a delivery and are used to protect their trailers from being tampered with during transit. Kevin snipped the thin strip of numbered metal, threw the handle and swung open the trailer doors. In the past three months Kevin had been here twice, once hitting a truck loaded with Kodak cameras and the second time offloading 40 cases of one-pound bags of peanut M&Ms. It was easy to sell cameras, and he had no problem getting paid for chocolate, but he had a decision to make as he looked into this trailer: walk away now or unload a few dozen cases of Janitor-In-A-Drum.

Tonight was a bust. Kevin had a rule to hit only one trailer a night and be in and out of the yard with all you could take in 10 minutes. He decided to walk away empty-handed. There was no sense in hauling a few dozen cases of Janitor-In-A-Drum back to the van if he knew he couldn't sell them. Better to leave tonight, hoping no one realizes the seal was broken, and come back next month to see what's available. He closed the doors to the trailer and waved to Bobby to follow him as they walked silently through the woods back to the Ford van with the Cadillac's plates.

While Kevin could afford to walk away empty-handed, Bobby needed to earn. As they drove away, Bobby told Kevin about tripling up on the Boston-Chicago game and losing $225 to three bookies, including The Syrian. He was ten days late, broke, and had been lying low, trying to buy time. He thought tonight was going to carry him. He didn't count on opening a trailer loaded with industrial strength liquid soap. Kevin told him to stay away from the track, keep out of the local bars and try to be invisible for a few days, until he had a chance to talk to The Syrian.

Kevin dropped Bobby off on the corner of Weeden Street and went back to the auto body to put away the van and return the plates to the Cadillac. He walked home, kissed his mother good night and went to bed.

The following day, Kevin drove to Central Falls to see what he could do. He explained that Bobby had gotten in way over his head on the Boston-Chicago game and asked The Syrian for time. The Syrian asked Kevin how Bobby planned to pay the other bookies, or if he was going to ask them for more time too. Before Kevin could speak, The Syrian put up his hand, signaling he didn't want Kevin to answer. The Syrian opened a drawer in his desk and pulled out cash. He gave Kevin $150, fifteen $10 dollar bills from a wrapped stack of 50, and he told him to go with Bobby in person to make sure Bobby paid the other two bookies. The Syrian told Kevin to tell Bobby there was no rush to pay back the $225 and that he owed the generous Syrian a favor. Kevin thanked his friend and took the cash.

As he listened to the sound of Kevin's footsteps walking down the two flights of stairs toward Dexter Street, The Syrian smiled, knowing he had just bought a man for $225.

Chapter 15

Kohl spent Saturday night alternating between getting hot over dancers in topless bars and looking at child pornography and S&M magazines in adult bookstores. He had no idea that he was being followed. He had no idea he was being watched, stalked, hunted like the young boys this predator had watched, stalked and hunted over the years.

It was late, after 1:30 in the morning, when he ordered his last drink. Finishing half, he left a few minutes later and stepped out into the summer heat of mid-August. He cruised Washington Street for about 20 minutes, trying to hook up with one of the many drunks who were trolling now that the bars were closed. Kohl was so pathetically predictable. His Saturday routine was unfolding this night exactly as it had each Saturday for the past four weeks. His predictability was going to be his downfall, because it allowed the people who sent Bobby downtown to know exactly what to expect.

Around 2 a.m. the human traffic came to a standstill and Kohl decided it was time to go home. He walked a few blocks to where he had parked his car each Saturday night for the past four weeks. He was staggering actually, with his walk, his speech, his vision, his judgment impaired from a night of drinking. He hadn't hooked up with anyone tonight, neither a previous sex partner nor an anonymous new friend. A block from his car, he smiled when he saw a guy leaning against a building on the dimly lit street. Kohl thought he might get laid after all. Men, women, young boys–Ronald Kohl wasn't picky when it came to consensual sex or sexual assault.

As Kohl slowed his walk, he was pleased to see that the guy was looking right at him. With eye contact established, Kohl was hoping the stranger would be interested in more than just conversation. It was past 2 a.m., and this guy was either selling dope or was here for sex–and Kohl had no interest in getting high.

When Bobby was sure it was Kohl, he reached into the doorway near where he was standing, grabbed the bat and swung. It was too late for Kohl to do anything about the baseball bat crashing into his left leg at the knee, shattering his kneecap and breaking his leg. It happened so fast Kohl felt nothing as his leg gave way and he collapsed onto his right knee. On one knee, kneeling on the sidewalk with his shattered left leg limp at his side, he was in no position to defend himself as a second swing of the 31 inch Del Crandall Louisville Slugger cracked his skull.

Kohl collapsed to the sidewalk without making a sound, other than the sounds that no one heard when his knee, leg and skull shattered. Two swings, eight seconds. No witnesses except the guy sitting alone in the old pickup truck 200 feet away in the parking lot, out of sight and all but invisible if not for the occasional glow from the lit end of his Dutch Master cigar. The man with the cigar saw the whole thing. He was supposed to. It had been planned that way. He sat patiently in the pickup, smoking his cigar, watching the street, watching Bobby, knowing Kohl would keep to his routine. It all went down as everyone expected, and Bobby had no idea he was being watched.

Bobby left Kohl lying face-up on the littered sidewalk as he walked to where he had parked his mother's car. He drove down Chapel, took a left on Matthewson and a right onto Fountain Street. His pulse was racing, sweat running down his chest, soaking his T-shirt. Thoughts were racing through his head. He was supposed to give Kohl a beating. Did he knock him out or kill him? Did anyone see him? Did he beat a man to death for $225 dollars? *I'll never bet again*, he told himself. Bobby felt like he was going to get sick.

He drove up Sabin Street, past the Civic Center, took a right onto Atwells Avenue across from the entrance to the Providence Police Station and headed north on 95. In a few minutes he'd be home with his nine week old $225 debt to The Syrian paid off in full. *But at what price?* Bobby wondered.

Kevin told Bobby two weeks ago that The Syrian no longer wanted the $225 he owed. There was only one way to clear the debt. The Syrian wanted Bobby to give Ronald Kohl a beating.

As Bobby stalked Kohl through the streets of Providence, cruising topless bars and adult bookstores, Bobby was himself being watched. It was for his own protection. Too many people had too much to lose if Bobby ran into any trouble doing what he needed to do.

The street was empty and scattered cloud cover blocked the light of the moon. No one heard the engine start on the dark green 1963 GMC four-wheel drive pickup parked 200 feet from where Kohl lay motionless on the sidewalk. The truck started through the abandoned parking lot and down the street without its headlights on. The driver could see Kohl's body lying across the sidewalk, covered in shadows cast from a nearby street light. The truck moved slowly up over the curb, putting the driver's side of the pickup onto the sidewalk. The front driver's side tire rolled over Kohl's body, crushing both hips, one at a time. As the steering wheel moved ever so slightly, the large rear tire rolled over his lower body, crushing both legs just below the knee. The driver put the pickup in reverse, backed up and slowly rolled over Kohl's body a second time. The rear tire exploded his rib cage, piercing his lungs with broken ribs, crushing his heart, his spleen and his appendix. The front tire rolled over his lower body, shattering the bones in his feet and both ankles. The man with the cigar wasn't done. One more time, up and over the body on the sidewalk. He puffed his cigar, put in the clutch, shifted from reverse to first gear and again slowly rolled over what remained of

Kohl, with the front and rear tires taking turns crushing his collar bone, both shoulders and bursting his skull.

Forward, reverse, forward. In less than a minute, the man with the cigar had crushed the life out of Ronald Thomas Kohl. Never again would he ever beat and rape another child.

Without stopping, the man with the cigar rolled the pickup truck off the sidewalk onto the street. He took another puff of his Dutch Master, turned on his headlights and drove the few blocks to Route 95, coming to a full stop at all traffic lights, using his blinker, driving under the speed limit and obeying the law all the way back to Lincoln. He needed to get to sleep soon. He'd be taking the kids to 7:30 Mass at St. Edward's in just a few hours.

Chapter 16

A Providence cop on routine patrol spotted something unusual as he drove down Snow Street. Using the spotlight on the driver's side of the patrol car, he lit up the sidewalk and saw Kohl's severely beaten and broken body. He glanced at his watch. It was 3 a.m. A little more than an hour had passed since the life had been crushed out of Kohl.

The cop could see from the comfort of his driver's seat that there was no need to rush to get out of his patrol car. He called in his location and requested that the Medical Examiner send a wagon and a body bag. *No need for an ambulance*, he thought. Whoever this had been, it was way too late for medical attention.

The phone woke Kevin. It was The Syrian asking if he would tow an old pickup truck to a junkyard. Kevin agreed and asked when it needed to be done. The Syrian said it was important that it be done today. Kevin never questioned The Syrian, so he hesitated before asking him if the junkyard would be open on a Sunday. The Syrian said the owner of the yard was waiting for the truck to be delivered. Kevin wrote down the address where he could find the pickup truck and assured The Syrian it would be towed before noon.

Kevin pulled ahead of the pickup and backed his tow truck to within a few feet of the front bumper. He set the hook and chain, secured the pickup and drove to a junkyard on the other side of Lincoln. It didn't take long for Kevin to strip the pickup of the transmission, carburetors, wheels, tires, battery and gas tank. Kevin watched as the forklift placed what was left of the dark green '63 GMC four-wheel drive pickup into the new E-Z Crusher. Within minutes the pickup was a flattened slab of metal less than three feet high. The remains of what used to be a pickup truck were loaded on a flatbed along with several other junk cars that had been crushed earlier in the week. Within a couple of hours the flatbed would be on its way to a recycler in southeastern Massachusetts, where crushed car scrap metal could be sold for a couple hundred dollars per ton.

On Monday, the detective investigating the case received fingerprints from the morgue and ran them through the Computerized Criminal History file. While there was

ID on the body when the Medical Examiner bagged the corpse, there was no way to visually confirm that the victim was the same guy in the photograph on the driver's license. They would have relied on an ID from a relative, but this guy was beaten so severely that he was unrecognizable. John Doe suffered massive trauma, unlike anything this seasoned detective had ever seen in his 16 years on the job. The vic's legs, pelvis and ribs had been broken. Pooled blood and considerable bruising in the chest and abdomen indicated severe internal organ damage. His head had been crushed and his lower jaw separated from his skull. Whoever he had been, he obviously pissed someone off. The detective felt sorry for the poor bastard.

When the fingerprints generated paper on John Doe, the detective's feelings for the victim quickly changed. Ronald T. Kohl, age 31. Addresses on Charles Street in North Providence, Rockwood Avenue in Cranston and Washington Street in Central Falls. Several previous arrests for Unnatural Sex Acts and sex crimes against children. Pleaded guilty to federal charges of using the mail for interstate sale of obscene material, shipped from his adult bookstore in Central Falls between September 1971 and November 1972. Convicted and sentenced to the Adult Correctional Institute (ACI) on his plea. After his release from the ACI, Kohl was again arrested for sex crimes against children. Currently pending trial after a recent Grand Jury indictment on multiple charges involving the abduction and rape of a 14-year-old boy from Lincoln in March of 1974.

This guy didn't learn did he? thought the detective. Too late now. Earlier feelings of pity for the poor bastard John Doe turned to contempt for the son-of-a-bitch, repeat offender, child-raping pornographer, Ronald T. Kohl. The detective thought about how much time this case would take. Someone beat the guy to death and the detective couldn't care any less. He got what was coming to him and the cops and the prosecutors had no interest in putting any time into finding out who killed this asshole low-life sex-crime felon. The detective knew he'd perform a cursory investigation at the scene of the murder and unless there were witnesses, this one would be shelved in the interest of Providence-style street justice. If the case could go 48 hours without a sloppy suspect or a nosey newspaper reporter, the file would be left on a shelf in the basement and ignored forever.

Chapter 17

My mother answered the phone. I knew something wasn't quite right when she called out, "Buddy, it's the police." My father took the call, which lasted less than a minute, then handed me a few bucks and asked me to go to Cumberland Farms to buy cigars and the Providence Journal. He didn't have to tell me there was something in the Journal the cops wanted him to see. In our house we read the Pawtucket Times, not the Providence Journal. What did the detective say that would make my father want to read today's Journal?

I rode my bike to the Cumberland Farms store a few hundred yards from our house. I got the Providence Journal and his cigars and began to thumb through the paper to see what was so important that the cops would call and my father would actually read a paper other than the Pawtucket Times.

The bold print headline read,

C.F. Man, 31, Beaten to Death in Providence

"Providence police said they are looking for witnesses in the beating death early Sunday morning of a 31-year-old Central Falls man. Police said the man, identified as Ronald T. Kohl, of Washington Street, died from severe head and internal injuries and a broken leg. Detectives said they have no information into the circumstances surrounding the attack on the Central Falls man. They said Kohl's body was taken to the state morgue for an autopsy to determine the exact cause of death."

I was physically shaking as I read the article. Tears leaked over my cheeks as I felt a sense of relief, security and safety, knowing this evil bastard no longer existed. Did he suffer? Was he scared? Did he feel alone and helpless as he was beaten? Did he beg for his life? Did he hope in vain for someone, anyone, to be on the street to help him? Did he feel any of the terror, fear or pain his young victims felt when he beat them, when he raped them? I found myself hoping so. The son-of-a-bitch was brutally beaten to death and the world was a safer, better place because of it. Never again would he be stalking boys in the vanilla suburbs of Providence. Never again would I run the risk of seeing him or his shitty little purple AMC Gremlin on Smithfield Avenue. Never again would I have to suffer the guilt or shame of retelling my story to the police, detectives, to blue-haired old ladies on a Grand Jury or in front of Kohl and his defense attorney in court. Ronald T. Kohl, who lived in Central Falls, who beat and raped me in Lincoln, was brutally beaten to death in the streets of Providence. His murder made the news. Case closed.

I got back on my ten-speed bike and saw Dennis coming out of the car wash. He knew what Kohl had done to me and like several other guys in my neighborhood, Dennis had looked out for me over the year and a half that had passed. They were always kind and protective, asking how I was doing, if I needed anything, if I was staying out of trouble. I felt safe being around the men in my town. These were good guys, bad guys, tough guys, street guys like Dennis, Jay, Tony, Mike, Paulie, Kevin and Danny. Guys that lived nearby, that worked nearby, owned local businesses, drank in local bars, guys that hung out at the basketball courts, guys that taught me how to box at the Boy's Club. They were guys that watched over me. Guys that let me know they were around to help if I ever needed it and that they wouldn't hesitate to straighten me out if I ever screwed up. They were friends of my father and my Uncle Mike, The Syrian. Some people, including the cops, had reason to believe they were bad men, but they were always good to me.

I rode up on Dennis as he was sitting in his Continental. I was out of control, literally shaking as I rode my bike. I rode fast to the driver's side of his car and blurted out, "He's dead, Dennis, he's dead."

Dennis looked at me and without hesitating, calmly said, "Don't say anything to anybody. There were a lot of people looking for this guy." I was frozen in place by the power of his words.

I never said who was dead. The newspaper story about Kohl's murder was just a few hours old. How did Dennis know it was Kohl I was talking about? How did he know who was dead, unless he did it, had it done, or knew who did? He never asked. He didn't have to. The word was out. Kohl's time was up.

Chapter 18

Over the past 35 years, I've been haunted by horrible, recurring memories of what Kohl did to me. It doesn't get easier over time. Long dead, he still visits me, silently sneaking up from out of nowhere, like a Trojan Horse, when I least expect it. From the grave, Ronald Kohl sits by my side on the couch every time the evening news reports a child abduction or sex crime. I don't watch *America's Most Wanted* or *Law and Order SVU*, because the stories are a catalyst, triggering long suppressed emotions, feelings, memories, fear and horror. TV crime dramas where the cops always get the bad guy offer little solace. Real life horror stories rip painful suppressed memories out from where they hide, from that recessed place in my brain that stores dark, dangerous, horrible memories. It happened when William Bonin confessed to abducting, raping and murdering 14 boys in California. When Jesse Timmendequas raped

and murdered Megan Kanka in New Jersey. When terror-
ists raped and murdered school children in Beslan. When
Ben Ownby, missing for four days, and Shawn Hornbeck,
missing for four years, were recovered in Missouri. When
Nancy Bochicchio and her daughter Joey were abducted
and murdered in Boca Raton.

Kohl visits me in my sleep. There have been dreams–
nightmares actually–dozens of them, about the rape and
my run home from his car. Sweat-inducing, thrashing-in-
my-sleep nightmares of hiding under the Ford Galaxie and
burrowing under the hedges to hide when I thought he was
tracking me down to kill me. Despite what happened that
night and the constant reminders that continue to haunt
me years later, I wouldn't change what happened. Kohl was
a serial predator, a violent pedophile who was trolling my
neighborhood in Lincoln, Rhode Island looking for young
boys. He beat me, raped me, and I stayed alive. I lived to
see him arrested, indicted and murdered. It might not have
turned out this way if he had grabbed one of my friends
or another kid in the neighborhood. Perhaps he'd still be
alive. Perhaps there would be dozens of more victims and
perhaps he would have progressed to the point of silencing
his victims by murdering them.

I've given little thought to his death over the years and a
lot of thought to the men that made my town safer because
of it. The Men in My Town. Masked men. Real men with
their true identities hidden like the imaginary Batman,
Superman, Spiderman and the Lone Ranger. Their identities protected by three decades of silence. Their silence and
mine. Silence driven by my wish to protect my protectors,
to eliminate the possibility that someone, someday, would

get arrested and perhaps go to jail for killing Kohl for what he did to me. Thirty-plus years of not saying anything to anyone out of respect for the Men in My Town and what they could do, what they did and the words of one who offered me comfort on a sunny August morning in 1975. "Don't say anything to anybody. There were a lot of people looking for this guy."

No one has ever been charged in connection with the beating death of Ronald T. Kohl.

Author's Note

Men in My Town is based on the true-life story of my abduction, beating and rape and the unsolved murder of the man who attacked me. The story is set in my hometown of Lincoln, Rhode Island, where I was attacked in 1974 and the gritty city of Providence, where my attacker was brutally beaten to death in 1975. It's a true story of someone getting away with murder.

Since the identity of the killer(s) and details of the actual murder are unknown, the manner in which the event is described in this book is pure fiction. It has to be.

While many of the places, events and men in this book are real, their names have been changed to protect the guilty and to conceal the identity of their innocent friends and relatives. Any similarity to real people, living or dead, is coincidental and not intended by the author.

Made in the USA
Lexington, KY
02 April 2010